Ski with the Big Boys

SKI
WITH THE
BIG BOYS

STU CAMPBELL

Photographs by Malcolm Reiss
Drawings by J. Duncan Campbell

Winchester Press

Copyright © 1974 by Stuart D. Campbell and Malcolm Reiss
All rights reserved

Library of Congress Catalog Card Number: 74–78702
ISBN: 0–87691–144–0

Book design by Mary Frances Gazze

Published by Winchester Press
460 Park Avenue, New York 10022

Printed in the United States of America

Contents

Preface

This is a book for those who really love skiing. It is not just for those who are already expert skiers—"expert" is a pretty vague term anyway—and nor is it for just anyone who skis. It is *not* meant for those who enjoy only those things which surround the sport, all of those fashionable social diversions which go along with (and go on *after*) skiing, but which are really no part of it.

It is not meant for "hot dog" skiers; it is not for racers, not for instructors. It is not for the ski-shop freak—the affluent guy so fascinated with the new developments in ski equipment that he will spend any amount of money on a gadget which promises to help him ski better. It is not for the cerebral skier—the guy who spends countless hours talking about *how* to do it, but rarely, if ever, actually goes out and *does* it. It is not for the technician—the skier (or instructor) who gets so bogged down in discussions of the physics or the "biomechanics" involved in turning a

pair of skis that he never really gives himself a chance to *feel* what it is like to carve rather than slide down the backside of an icy mogul.

This is a book for *skiers*—for people who want to do, to watch, to sense, and most important, to appreciate skiing.

Skiing beyond the level of mere proficiency—a "proficient" skier

FIGURE 1: In spite of all its commercialism, in spite of all the clichés which surround it, skiing remains winter's most soulful pastime. Alone at the end of a snowy day the skier's form is nearly lost in the background of dark trees, self-expression transcends technique, and there is totally silent communication with the mountainside.

might describe himself as "able to get down anything"—begins to become an art form. Like any art form, it defies complete analysis. Expert skiing, in spite of what instructors and ski writers have been trying to make of it for years, is far more than putting together a series of isolated motions in the right place at the right time. The great skier has a nearly indefinable quality about him which transforms his downhill progress into something which is a great deal more than a bunch of "good moves." The speed, the subtle relationship between the skis and the always changing snow, the relaxed flow of the body over rough terrain, the apparently instinctive choice of line, and a myriad of other factors all combine to create a kind of ballet on snow, a disciplined and at the same time free expression of personality and style, a sense of precariously balanced and dangerously fragile harmony with the hostile side of a mountain.

Skiing, when all other descriptions fail, is motion. To reduce it—as do so many books about skiing—to a sequence of static, posed positions is to render it meaningless. As in any art form, it is the total effect of the work which is most important. When one particular aspect of a skiing maneuver is isolated so that it can be discussed and understood, the totality and fluidity of the thing is lost or, at best, suspended. At the same time any real knowledge of what is happening is impossible without a *certain* amount of dissection. So the components must be recognized without destroying the essence.

At this point it might be a good idea to make a distinction between *technique* and *style*. Skiing is a highly personal physical and mental exercise. For the expert skier, creativity and individuality take over where technique leaves off. A skier's *style* is how he uses and arranges the various aspects of technique which are available to him. A very good skier is one who has lots of technical possibilities in his bag of tricks that he can use in any given situation. Building a large repertoire of things to do when the terrain or the surface of the snow call for it is largely a matter of lots of experience, and even more a matter of lots and *lots* of skiing mileage.

Technique, then, is simply whatever works. If a particular set of related motions seems to work well for most skiers in most situations, this series of motions can be regarded as good technique—not style. Techniques can be combined and blended together to form one's skiing style. Much of skiing literature tends to regard technique as an end in itself. It's not. Style is. Skiing's ultimate end should be artistry—style based on good, sound technical principles. A good ski teacher's job is to explain and demonstrate technique. He must realize, as you the reader must recognize, that it is no teacher's function to dictate style. Style is *your* thing.

The very best skiing styles, like the very best designs, always seem to be the most simple. "Simplicity," in fact, should set the tone for this entire book. Very good skiers admire other very good skiers who use no excessive, nonfunctional, exaggerated motion in their skiing. The very best skier is never a showboat. He rarely, if ever, does anything flamboyant. He may never seem to do anything particularly spectacular. Because everything he does relates directly to the snow and to what he is trying to accomplish on the snow, because he is not directly interested in impressing someone who might be watching from the chairlift, his skiing, ironically enough, is the most beautiful, the most noticeable, the most spectacular of all.

Ski teachers who do not "show and tell" *simply* are self-defeating. A book which is so technical that its author seems to have forgotten that skiing is supposed to be beautiful and supposed to be fun is missing the point as badly as a ski instructor who talks only of joints, muscles and bones. We have a great deal to learn from the great technicians, coaches and racers of the world. But there is no reason why we should be asked to suffer through their egotistical pedantics and complicated diagrams and formulae, or to tolerate their expressions of nationalistic chauvinism.

There seems to be a need for a different book: a simple book written for good skiers who like to ski more than they like to read about it; a book which is not laden with complicated nomenclature and technical jargon; a book by someone who is actually out there on the side of the mountain *doing* it all day seven days a week all winter long. It is time for someone to say something about what *really* works out there, instead of speculating about what *should* work.

Ski with the Big Boys is written and illustrated in what is hoped is the most simple and interesting way possible. It consists of short chapters with brief comments at the beginning of each. Most of the text is based on questions which have actually been asked by perceptive students in advanced ski lessons. (I wrote them all down on crumpled 3x5 cards which I carried in my pocket for several winters.) The questions are followed by discussion, answers and illustrations. You may choose not to read the book from cover to cover. You may want to read only those sections which apply to you. Sometimes the questions will seem to be answered in more than one way. There is, after all, more than one way to turn on a mogul. Sometimes the answers will be traditional ski-school answers, because these answers are valid and useful ones. Later, newer, more refined and more efficient solutions are offered. We must always bear in mind that ski technique is constantly evolving, but that new developments in technique do not necessarily *replace* what has worked well before. New developments offer a choice, broaden one's skiing personality, and increase the size of your bag of tricks.

Because this book is for people who are interested in skiing on a relatively sophisticated level, it begins where many skiing manuals end: with parallel skiing. We must never minimize the importance of those skiing fundamentals learned so carefully at the beginning and intermediate levels of skiing. This book will frequently make reference to the snowplow and the snowplow turn as positions from which many of the sport's more advanced maneuvers develop. But skiing at these lower levels is more than adequately covered in other sources. In spite of what others may say, and what so many may think, parallel skiers are not yet expert skiers. Everything that comes before it is just preparation. The parallel turn marks the point where skiing really begins.

—*Stu Campbell*
Stowe, Vermont

Spring 1974

Ski with the Big Boys

1 *Stance*

Before you do anything, program yourself to stop looking like a ski instructor! Ski instructors, because they get into exaggerated positions to
demonstrate a point to a student, are the greatest "posers" in the world. If
you watch ski instructors for very long, you might get the impression that
skiing is little more than getting from one awkward pose to another
equally contorted position as quickly as possible. The old "reverse shoulder" and "comma position"—if you don't even know what these are, it is
just as well—did a lot to reinforce this impression. So did still-poster pictures of Stein Eriksen swooping down easy open slopes.

Any ski instructor who is also a very good skier—and not all of them
are, as you have no doubt noticed—never gets caught posing when he goes
out to ski just for fun. Suddenly in the bumps, on the ice, or in the
"crud," the "proud peacock" positions vanish. He knows that any skier
who allows himself to get into static, "elegant" positions when he is trying

1

to ski the really tough stuff just does not survive. When you decide that it is time for *you* to go out and ski with the big boys, you had better make up your mind that there is no time—and no space sometimes—for posing on expert terrain.

How you choose to stand on your skis is, of course, entirely up to you. There are probably as many styles of standing still as there are skiers. It is wrong to try to make everyone look exactly alike, as some ski schools have tried to do in the past. So without trying to alter whatever is *your* normal skiing stance too much, try to keep two principles in mind:

1. *Allow all of the joints in your legs and upper body to flex forward.* This will make you feel that you are standing in a sort of slouch. If you feel a little like an ape, this is good. This "gorilla stance," as we may as well call it, doesn't look especially nice—that's for sure. But try to remember that what feels different is not necessarily bad. Because you are bent at the waist and your back is relaxed and rounded, you are in a great position to make adjustments in your body as the surface beneath the skis changes.

2. *Always try to keep the upper body* (and think of the hips as part of the upper body) *facing the way you are going.* Instead of trying to keep your upper body parallel with the line of the skis (you may once have been taught this position), keep it "square" or perpendicular to the line the skis are taking. The "reverse-shoulder-counter-rotated-comma" position is not only unnatural and inefficient, it will give you a backache if you really try to do it all day long.

When you are driving a car you probably don't arch your back. You don't normally turn and face your passenger. You don't turn and face out the side window. You face the way you are going: out the windshield! It is ironic that often rank beginners stand on their skis better than do many ski-school-trained experts.

STANCE

What's so great about the way a beginner stands on skis?

Sometimes a lot. We can learn from him if he is normally built and normally coordinated. Because he is a little apprehensive about his very first run down a gentle slope, he is likely to stand in a very good position. There is nothing too casual, too static, or too posed about his initial posture. He bends forward at the waist (sometimes *too* much) and keeps adjusting his upper body and head to keep his balance. He should have been told to keep his knees and ankles bent. As he moves down the hill, he assumes a kind of "natural athletic stance."

"Natural athletic stance!" He looks like a Neanderthal man!

Forget the ski-instructor look for a moment. Suppose you are standing on the baseline of a tennis court waiting for an opponent to ram a service down your throat. You probably would not be standing "straight and proud." If you *did,* the serve would be past you before you had a chance at it. To be ready for an approaching ball you would be in a "natural athletic stance."

Watch other athletes: a forward waiting for a tap in basketball, a defensive back waiting for a snap, a center awaiting a face-off in hockey, a shortstop expecting a line drive . . . or a very good skier approaching a bump at high speed. All of them are awaiting motion. They are standing on the balls of their feet, they are slouched in the upper body, their hands and arms are lowered and slightly ahead. The eyes are focused on what is coming.

But I don't want to look like a gorilla! Skiing is a proud sport. Why do I have to look like an ape?

You don't *have* to, of course. Stand in whatever position you think looks good for as long as you can get away with it. But when the terrain starts to demand it, you are probably going to have to slouch more and bring your hands farther forward. Like it or not, it is the only way you are going to have a fighting chance of skiing well.

If the "gorilla stance" is so repugnant to you that you cannot accept it at all, even after studying the stances of lots of very good skiers, then maybe you are not *really* interested in true expert skiing at all. If your goal is to stay on the intermediate slopes and *look* nice, then some of the stuff in the rest of this book may not be for you.

All right. Should I make any effort to keep my feet together?

We have already noticed how athletes in different sports look surprisingly similar in their expectation of motion. All of them have their feet apart and their toes pointed slightly inward—pigeontoed.[1] In skiing this is obviously the very stable snowplow position, which as pretty good skiers already, we are not concerned with.

"Parallel skiing" simply means that both skis are going in the same direction. Too many people think that skiing "parallel" means that the feet must be right together. For a few skiers having the feet tight together

---

[1] Horst Abraham, *P.S.I.A. American Technique Manual,* supplement (Denver: Professional Ski Instructors of America, 1972), p. 17.

may be the most natural and comfortable position. For most of us, though, the most comfortable thing is to have our feet 4 to 8 inches apart and still parallel. For others it may be more like 10 to 16 inches apart. Whatever is good for *you* is probably fine. Keep in mind that it is difficult for women, most of whom have wider hips than men, to stand with their knees, ankles and feet locked tight together.

Do women, because they are built differently, have to develop a different technique?

No, I don't think so. I have worked with nearly as many women as I have men. Women who have progressed to the point of being advanced skiers—and there are too few of them, I'm sorry to say—can be taught in exactly the same way as men. They learn just as well, and there seems to be little or nothing that they cannot do as far as actual skiing is concerned. In fact, because on the average they are not as strong physically as male skiers and are unable to use a lot of brute force, they often compensate by becoming better *technical* skiers than many men.

There are a few real experts around who are trained in "biomechanics," which is the study of the human body and how it functions in terms of its skeletal structure, musculature, joints, and so forth. They tend to believe that ski technique is frequently "male specific." That means that it is designed by men *for* men, and that as a result there are many things which women, because of their different anatomy, find very difficult.

I have found that this is usually not the case. Nearly everything I say in this book applies equally to both men and women. I make no distinctions, except in a few instances such as keeping the feet locked tight together—which is harder for women. In other words, when I say "you," I am not talking about men only. When I say "he," I could just as easily be saying "he or she."

Are there any advantages to having the feet together?

Not really. It looks nice, and as you become more and more confident, your feet will probably come closer and closer together. Keeping the feet together was done originally for technical as well as stylistic reasons. It was thought—to oversimplify—that if the feet could be close together, the skis could be made to operate as a single unit. Racers soon began to realize, though, that an "open" or "wide-track" stance was not only more stable, but allowed the feet and legs to work independently like the "independent front suspension" on a car.

In the only slightly more awkward widened stance, the weighting of the skis is still the same. It also allows us to edge *both* skis instead of only the downhill ski. Two edges are better than one when it gets really slippery.

I often find myself wanting to look at my feet when I am skiing. Is this bad?

It sure is! And not just because you cannot see where you are going. If you have ever had riding instruction, you were probably told never to look at the horse. If you do, you get behind the action of the animal. It is sort of the same thing on skis.

It is normal to be interested in what your feet and your skis are doing. For instance, you might be concerned about the tips of your skis crossing. Believe it or not, one of the easiest ways to make your tips cross is to look at them. If you are built like me—and like most people—you have to move your stomach back out of the way to see your feet. *This* makes your fanny stick out, which puts ankle pressure on the backs of the boots rather than on the fronts. If there is no pressure against the fronts of the boots, you are not able to control what the tips are doing. It is almost

6

as though they were free to do as they please. They may cross, or worse, go off in opposite directions! That is why it is important to *feel* what your feet are doing so you don't need to look down.

What should I be feeling in my feet?

You should feel that you are standing on the entire length of your feet, with slightly more weight on the balls of your feet than on the heels. You should *not* feel as though you are standing on your toes! If everything feels right along the soles of your feet, you should then be conscious of the pressure against the fronts of your ankles. If you can't feel it, bend your knees and ankles more. This is why your boots are so big and stiff and uncomfortable: so you can push against them and control the tips. Don't worry at first about the rest of the ski. In your car you are concerned mostly about what the front wheels are doing. The back ones—and the tails of the skis—take care of themselves.

I've been told that in my normal stance I stick my fanny out too much. I see why this is bad, but how can I keep it in?

If your are a lady, keep reminding yourself to "look sexy." Every woman knows what this means. Men don't so much. While you are skiing, pretend that for some reason you want to look especially alluring. "Tuck" your pelvis, pulling your fanny and your tummy in at the same time. If you "look sexy" you are probably in a great skiing position.

If you are a man and *your* fanny sticks out—a common problem even with good skiers—thrust your pelvis forward so that your hips are in a line above—but not *behind*—your feet. If you let your hips "get behind," you can bend your knees all you like, and still be unable to apply enough pressure to the fronts of the boots. When this is the case, you are literally out of control. Be careful, though. Don't push your hips so far forward that you are straightening your back too much.

You say that it is important to be facing the way I am going. I have learned otherwise, but what you say makes good sense. Is there anything I can do to make sure I am facing ahead instead of downhill?

Easy. Always try to keep your hands in front of you. Get your arms into a comfortable position and then put your hands where you can see them both. If both hands are *always* at least within your peripheral vision—and you are looking the way you are going—your upper body has to be facing the right way.

If you lose sight of one hand, you are posing. In a *left* turn, for instance, if you lose sight of the inside hand (the uphill hand as you complete the turn), you have let your body rotate too much and are turned facing out the side window of the imaginary car. If you lose sight of the outside hand, it is as if you have turned to face your passenger. You are too counter-rotated.

Is this "gorilla stance" really going to help me on rough terrain?

Let's face it, rough terrain is what expert skiing is all about. This is why there is a whole chapter devoted just to stance. In this "natural athletic position" you can let your body act like an accordion. As you ski over sharp bumps, your body should want to fold (see Fig. 3). Your head

FIGURE 2: *The $100 ski lesson.* Professional skiers—like anyone else—occasionally fall into bad habits. Last year I was having some trouble with my own skiing. For help I turned to an older instructor and coach whom I respect a lot. "Let's go out and have a look," he said.

Like all great ski teachers, he needed to watch my skiing for only about ten seconds before he recognized the problem. "You're letting your left hand get too far back," he said, "so your upper body is getting out of square with your skis."

"I don't believe you," I said. "I can see the hand all the time."

"I don't think so," he said. "I'll show you." He fastened his ski poles around my waist like this, and made me ski again. Sure enough, in about every third turn to the right my left hand would drift back far enough so that my pole would *click* against his. I was convinced and my skiing problem was solved—at least until the next one developed.

"That'll be one hundred dollars," he said. I refused to pay my grinning friend, but I have used his simple exercise many times since then to persuade other skiers that they need to move their hands farther in front of them. Once they eliminate the click they ski better.

9

FIGURE 3: *Straight run over rough terrain.* This drawing illustrates *avalement*—terrain swallowing—in its most simple form. Let your eyes run across the drawing from left to right to get a feeling for what is happening. See how all the joints in the body absorb the bump? The head stays at more or less the same level as the body collapses beneath it.

1. This is the demonstrator's "natural athletic stance" on skis. His knees and ankles are bent. His back is rounded, his eyes are looking ahead and are level, and his head is not tilted. Both his hands are low to provide balance and are within the field of vision. This means that the upper body is facing the way he is going.

2. As the bump approaches the "gorilla stance" becomes more pronounced. The hips are directly above the feet, which means that the skier should feel that his weight is evenly distributed along the entire length of his feet. As the ski tips begin to climb the bump he will feel gentle pressure against his toes.

3. As the body starts to fold the demonstrator automatically pushes his feet slightly ahead. This permits the body to collapse more easily. If you isolate this picture from the sequence—a favorite trick of many ski photographers—the skier *appears* to be sitting back because his hips are behind his feet. But remember that

he is skiing uphill at this point! More important: see how the knee is well ahead of the ankle. He still has all kinds of forward pressure against the ski boot.

4. By the time he has reached the top of the mogul the center of the skier's body mass has caught up so that it is directly above the feet again. This is the point of maximum body "compression." It has sometimes been called the "squatty-body" position.

5. As the "bottom drops out" on the backside of the bump, the body must unfold or "extend" itself again to keep the skis on the snow.

(Continued next page)

6. And the natural athletic stance appears again.

Don't forget: At low speeds *avalement* is almost passive. The arrows in the drawing seem to force the folding of the body.

At higher speeds—and in more difficult bumps—*avalement* becomes more active. The skier will consciously retract his legs and roll his upper body forward to keep from being thrown into the air at the crest of the bump, and then actively extend himself again—pushing his feet into the "hole" on the back side of the mogul.

In advanced skiing on expert terrain the name of the game is constant snow-ski contact!

will stay at the same level while the body seems to collapse and come up underneath your head. At the point when you are most collapsed, you will practically be in a fetal position. Then the body will start to unfold again on the opposite side of the bump.

An accordion with any major section that does not fold is worthless. If you keep your back too straight and stiff by not allowing yourself to bend at the waist, you are not taking full advantage of your body's ability to curl up and get into what a gymnast would call a "tucked position."

What is the point of all this?

That's really the basic question, isn't it? One of the goals for all good skiers should be to ski smoothly over any terrain. This "Neanderthal" stance allows us to reduce and even eliminate small bumps and "washboard" by taking up the shock in our joints. *This* allows us to keep our skis in contact with the snow. We will see how important this is in Chapter 6, "Big Moguls." Most important, as we shall see, the "gorilla stance" will allow us to *use* irregularities in the terrain. In the old stiff stance it is too easy, at high speed, to be bounced around by bumps. If you can stop skiing like a demonstrating instructor, *you* at least have the potential to dictate what is going to happen to yourself on the snow.

12

2 *Parallel Turns*

Lots of people who ski with their skis parallel, or *think* they ski with their skis parallel, are not making good parallel turns. Everyone seems to be in such a hurry to ski with his feet together that few spend enough time learning how to do it right. Lots of people who are still doing stem christies, in fact, ski much better technically than do people who are self-taught parallel skiers or products of "instant parallel" ski schools. There are few short cuts to knowing how to make strong, effectual parallel turns.

Two things make it possible for us to make an elementary turn with our skis parallel: (1) some sort of *lifting action* which makes us momentarily light, combined with (2) some sort of *twisting force* or torque, which will be discussed shortly.

If you have ever stood on your bathroom scale at home, you may already know how this "lifting action" works. If you bent your knees as though getting ready to jump off the scale, and then snapped your legs to a position that was more or less straight—but *without* actually jumping—you found that you could make the needle on the scale bounce downward anywhere from 70 to 100 pounds. By bouncing even gently, you can lower your weight considerably every time your body has gone *up*. If you are too fat, it is too bad that this momentary lightness is so brief. In skiing it is too bad too. We must take very quick advantage of it or we have lost it.

The parallel turn, then, consists of three motions. The most important one, in many ways, is the middle one, the lifting motion or "up" motion as we say. This "up" motion is what is called "unweighting"—"*up* unweighting," to be a little more precise.

But it is impossible to make an "up" motion from a position that is already "up"—you have nowhere to go. The first motion in a parallel turn, at least when you are first learning, must be a "down" motion. What comes up should go down first. The third motion in the turn, the motion after unweighting, is another *down*, where the knees drive forward and in the direction of the turn—very much the way they do in the snowplow turn. Down . . . up . . . and down again; that's all it takes.

If you are serious about learning to make *effective* parallel turns, spend some time at it. Choose your terrain carefully. A wide smooth hill is ideal. Don't choose one that is too flat, or one that is uncomfortably steep for you. You should find a place where you can ski safely in the fall line— the line a ball would take if it were to roll straight down the hill—from 20 or 30 yards without worrying about going too fast. Allow yourself a morning by yourself to concentrate on what you are doing.

How do I begin?

Start all of your maneuvers from the fall line. Point your skis straight down the hill and make one turn to the right, for example. Stop, and make the same turn—from the fall line—to the left. At first you will be making what is roughly a 90-degree turn. If you traverse first—a "traverse" is what we do when we ski *across* the hill—and then try to make a turn all the way into the opposite traverse, you are going to have to make a turn which is close to 180 degrees. This is too much to begin with. Make snow-plow turns first.

Snowplow turns? Why do I have to do that? I've never even understood why people have to learn to snowplow turn at all.

The snowplow turn is probably more important than you think. The same things that make it possible to make a snowplow turn make it possible to make a parallel turn.

Stand in the snowplow position for a moment with your skis pointing right down the fall line. Notice that you very conveniently have one ski that points off in one direction and one ski that points off in the other. If you ski straight down the hill in this snowplow, and then start to "steer" a little with the foot on the ski that is already pointed the way you want to go—by turning your foot so that the toes point to the inside even more than they already are—you will start to change direction slightly. Now put lots of weight on that same ski and *push* the knee forward and toward the direction the ski is pointing (see Fig. 4).

I turned. So what? A beginner can learn to do that in an hour.

Yes, some beginners can. But you would be amazed at the number of so-called "parallel" skiers who have never felt what you just felt. By weighting the outside ski—in the snowplow this is the one that's pointed

15

FIGURE 4: *Snowplow turn with foot and leg steering.* The *carved* snowplow or "wedge" turn is a fundamental move from which most of skiing's more sophisticated maneuvers develop. The foot and leg motions are almost exactly the same as those seen in advanced parallel turns. Compare the action of the skier's left leg in this sequence to the action of his left leg in Fig. 5. Both of these turns were made in exactly the same spot.

1. This is the very stable snowplow or "braking-wedge" position. The body is in a "natural athletic stance" similar to the one in Fig. 3. All joints are flexed: the hands are held forward and low. The tips of the skis are together; the tails apart. Each ski is on its inner edge.

2. One ski—in this case the left one—is already pointing the way the skier wants to go.

3. He steers with the foot on the ski that points in the direction of the turn. The motion is a little like grinding out a cigarette with his foot. Take a look at the left leg. It has done nothing yet. The demonstrator has *initiated* the turn and altered his course simply by turning his left foot to the inside.

4. Now the leg begins to steer. The left knee is pushed "down and in." This puts that ski more on edge and applies pressure on its tip. It must begin to carve at that point.

5. Can you see how *both* legs appear to be steering here? Both knees have moved forward and to the left. The left leg causes the turning ski to keep carving. The right knee causes the other ski to flatten on the snow, letting it turn more easily.

6. The legs steer the skis well out of the fall line until . . .

7. . . . . the skier comes to a stop.

16

PARALLEL TURNS

where you want to go—and by pushing that outside knee "down and in" you are doing two things: (1) you are automatically putting that ski on its edge, and (2) you are pressing against the tip of the ski. Because of the strange way the ski is shaped, it will "carve" a turn when you do this. It is irresistible. The ski will do it every time.

Practice feeling what it is like to make "carved"—not slipping— snowplow turns in both directions. This leg action is the same "twisting force" that is used in the parallel turn.

How is this the same in the parallel turn?

Feel the motion one more time as you are standing still in the snow- plow. Push the knee down and to the inside. Now put your skis parallel al- though not necessarily together. Now push *both* knees down and in. The action is the same whether your legs are apart or together.

Stand in a fairly high "gorilla stance" and point your parallel skis down the fall line. Ski ahead with most of your weight on your left ski— this will be your *outside* ski as you make a turn to the right. As you pick up a little speed, sink down, aggressively driving both of your knees to the right. If you are pushing forward against the boots, both skis will turn to the right. This is called an "uphill christie" (see Fig. 5). If you turn far enough you will come to a stop. Repeat it, turning to the left.

I feel it. But what about the "down-up" part?

We have approached the parallel turn backward—talking about the third motion (the *second* "down" first). If you can feel how your legs, knees, and feet can work together to "torque" your skis out of the fall line, it is time to start back at the beginning.

Start in the fall line again in the same high stance. You are going to

18

make any sort of a half-baked turn to the right. What the turn itself looks like does not matter. As you ski, sink down *without* trying to make any sort of turn. You should feel yourself sinking by bending the knees and dropping the whole body like a plumb bob. Don't just drop your fanny. That will make you sit back. Remember: the only reason you are sinking down now is so you can come up.

Once you are "down," make an "up" motion. *Then* sink down again and try to do what you did with your knees and feet when you made the uphill christie. Everything is not going to work perfectly at first! All you should be concerned with is the initial "down."

Why so much emphasis on the first down motion? I don't see very good skiers doing it.

Don't be deceived by the very good skier. His unweighting motion may be so subtle that it is almost imperceptible. His skis seem to be turning by themselves as if by magic. You must believe that the unweighting is still there. It is. The very good skier is good at hiding it. Don't forget: he may have been skiing ever since he could walk, and has a lot more "feel" for his skis than you do. He uses as little "down-up" as he can get away with.

You should be exaggerating the down motion for one simple reason. If you sink down more, you can come up more! The more faith you have in your ability to come up and make yourself lighter, the easier it is going to be to make turns. People who do not have faith in their ability to "unweight" cheat a little before each turn by stemming—giving the outside ski a head start on the turn. A stem is half a snowplow—not parallel. You will see people doing this all over every mountain.

FIGURE 5: *Uphill christie across the fall line.* An uphill christie is also done with foot and leg steering. The aggressive driving of the legs forces a "down" motion. (Look at the contrast in height of stance between #3 and #6.) This downward movement in which the knees also move laterally—in the direction of the turn—is the same in the completion of all parallel turns.

1. This maneuver should first be tried either right in the fall line or from a very steep traverse, as the demonstrator is doing here. A very "flat" traverse—*across* the hill—will make it more difficult because you will have that much farther to turn. When you try it, keep your skis parallel, though not necessarily together.

2. Notice the high stance. But remember: "high" never means that the legs are straightened entirely and the knee joints locked.

3. Here the skier has begun to shift some of his weight to his left ski—the outside one as the turn progresses.

4. Because he is standing directly over the skis' pivot point he can begin steering with his feet. The skis, as you can see, are still relatively "flat" on the snow (more so than in the last three figures, for example). This turn—like the snowplow turn—is started at the point of the body which is in closest contact with the snow. In other words, the turn starts at the bottom—in the feet.

5. As the legs take over the job of steering the skis are more on edge.

6. See how much edging is going on here? The legs are more bent than at the same stage in the snowplow turn (see Fig. 4) because this turn—done in the exact tracks made by the snowplow turn—involves a lot more speed.

7. This "christie" is completed to the point where the skis turn back uphill and come to a stop.

One other interesting point: The demonstrator started in a wide-track stance, but because he was standing with most of his weight on the turning outside ski, centrifugal force helped to move the inside ski closer to the outside one, bringing the feet closer together. The moral here may be this: don't try to put your feet together and then try to make everything work from that stance! Practice enough so that you can do the maneuver correctly, and your skis will *naturally* come closer and closer together.

20

1

2

3

4

5

6

7

21

FIGURE 6: *Wide-track parallel—cramponnage.* Lots of skiers who are just getting into parallel learn very quickly if they are taught the "big-toe/little-toe" approach. Here we see the demonstrator standing in an open stance—with his feet quite far apart. He is thinking about putting most of his weight on the big toe of his right foot and the rest of his weight on the little toe of his left foot. Positioning the weight this way very naturally causes both skis to be put on edge—in this case to the uphill side.

Any reasonable athletic skier who can understand this can be taught to make more or less parallel turns on very easy terrain, with a minimum of unweighting, by simply changing edges and steering—feeling the weight distribution change from "big toe, little toe" to "little toe, big toe."

Using the edges of both skis is far more effective than using just one. Very good skiers—and some intermediate skiers who have practiced wide-track parallel— tend to ski slightly bowlegged sometimes, like the skier in this photo. The "hooking" inside knee (the uphill knee) is the result of the skier's wanting to put that ski on edge too. Look at photographs of racers doing exactly this. The French feel that this is a very important move and have attached a name to this very effective edging of the uphill ski. They call it *cramponnage*—"hanging on."

PARALLEL TURNS

Shouldn't I be doing something with my pole?

Yes, you should. The pole plant comes just as you make this first down motion. It becomes an important timing device which "triggers" the up motion. To initiate the turn you should feel yourself sink down and plant your pole all in the same motion. Plant the right pole for right turns, the left pole for left turns. If it is hard for you to remember right from left quickly, as it is for me, think about planting the inside pole. The pole is not something to lean and pivot on, so don't even try.

Is there a "correct" way to plant the pole?

We get dangerously close to dictating style when we start to pick on somebody's pole plant. You *do* have a couple of choices. You can plant your pole so that the palm of your hand is "open." This means that the palm is facing forward. This looks very nice. But notice how this puts your elbow very close to your torso. Each time you ski past your planted pole, you risk bumping into your elbow and knocking yourself backward and off balance. This is obviously not a good technique for steep terrain.

The simplest pole plant is the best. Reach out to plant your pole as if you were about to shake hands with someone—fingers forward instead of palm forward. This puts your arm in a little more natural position, with your elbow a little bit farther away from your body. On the other hand, don't look like you are carrying a watermelon under each arm. Try not to let your poling hand pass in front of your body before the pole is planted. This is an affectation. Always keep both hands outside the outside edge of each ski.

23

Where should I plant the pole?

It would be great if there were some neat formula such as "plant the pole 3⅝ inches back from the right tip on a 45-degree angle." Some instructors have said, "Plant your pole halfway between the tip of the ski and the toe of your boot." Suggestions like this are not especially helpful. Where you plant your pole depends on how fast you are going, what position you are standing in, and how long your poles are—if they are longer than 2–3 inches above the waist when they are in the snow, they are much too long for modern skiing.

The faster you are traveling, the farther ahead you will want to plant the pole. As a rule of thumb, plant your pole far enough ahead so that you feel yourself being pulled forward against your boots as the hand reaches out. If you reach *too* far forward, you can throw your shoulders out of "square." Plant your pole anywhere in the pie-shaped area between the tips and an imaginary line which would pass through both feet and extend to either side (see Fig. 7).

I understand the importance of the down motion and the pole plant. Now what about the up?

As you make your "up" motion, remember that your skis are pointing down a slope—they are not horizontal. This is, after all, what alpine skiing is all about. If you make an up motion which is vertical, or nearly vertical, you are going to be sitting *back* against the boots. When this happens, as we have already learned, the skis want to accelerate out from under you just at this very critical point in the turn.

To prevent this unsteadiness, you are going to have to come up and *forward* each time. If this is difficult for you to understand or seems a little bit scary, stick your chin out as you come up. If you lead with your chin,

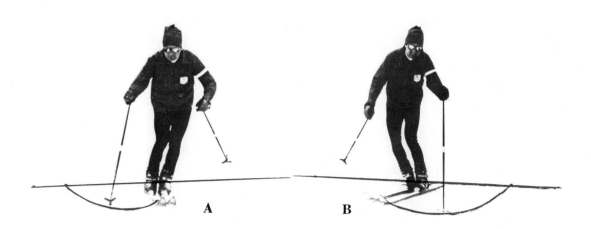

A   B

FIGURE 7: *Pole plant.* The pole plant should be as simple and unaffected as possible. It is just like reaching out to shake someone's hand.

In a parallel turn with up motion, the pole should be planted far enough forward (A) so that you can feel yourself being pulled forward against the boots as you make your initial down motion to enter the turn. Be careful not to reach *so* far forward that you throw your shoulders out of square with the skis.

There are no strict rules about where the pole should be planted—so long as the plant never occurs *behind* the feet! If you were to draw an imaginary line through the insteps of both feet which extended for about four feet to either side of you, and then drew an imaginary arc to the tips of the skis (B), you would have outlined the area in which a pole plant might be made.

As a general rule, as you go faster you will plant your pole farther ahead. As the slopes gets steeper, the pole will be planted farther back from the tips and farther down the hill (B again). Do you see how this tends to twist the upper body in the direction of the turn? This is called "anticipation," which is explained in Chapter 4.

as though inviting someone to take a swing at you, you will be unweighting better, and won't feel that by coming forward so much you are going to fall on your nose. Once you feel what it is like to be unweighting forward, hold your head in a more normal position.

Should I hop the tails of my skis off the snow?

Only as a last resort. Some instructors "hop" the tails to "displace" them away from the direction of the turn, and to exaggerate what happens when you unweight the skis. But these same guys rarely hop when they ski for fun. The "hop" is just a teaching device—a means to a more fluid end. For most people a good "down-up" is more than enough.

Sometimes I come up and forward and nothing happens! What's the problem?

The skis are not going to turn by themselves. Remember: the only reason you went down in the first place is so that you could come up. You come *up* only to unweight. Neither of these motions has anything to do with changing direction. They are just preparatory motions. Unweighting *combined* with torque—"down and in" knee crank—causes the turn to happen.

Remember this too: the lightness on the bathroom scale was ever so brief. If you come up too straight—so that the knees lock—or if you stay up too long, you have lost the lightness. How often have you heard instructors yelling at students, "Down . . . up . . . down!"? That's not really quite right. You can stay down as long as you like, but you cannot stay up! Once you come up, you are committed to the turn. It *should* sound more like, "Down . . . updown!" Can you hear the difference?

26

PARALLEL TURNS

Which ski leads?

The uphill ski—the inside ski as you are turning—is the one that leads. When the weight shifts to the outside ski, the lead changes to the inside ski. But this should not be something that you spend a lot of time thinking about. When people skied with their feet locked tight together, leading with one ski was more important. The only reason for keeping one ski ahead was to prevent the skis from crossing. The "open stance" reduces the chances of this happening somewhat. A very slight lead is enough.

Try not to shuffle one foot so far ahead that the downhill knee gets "tucked" behind the uphill knee. This is a common error, and is one of those bad, inefficient, static positions. It takes much too long to "untuck" the knees, change the lead, and "retuck" the knees again. You have enough to worry about besides that! Sometimes people "tuck" one knee to get the downhill ski on edge more. As a result they look like they are waterskiing on a single ski, with all—or at least too much—of their weight on the *heel* or the back foot. If you need more edge, bend both knees. Allow your knees to move past each other freely.

I have gone down so I can come up. I have come up and made myself light, and then sunk down driving my knees in the direction of the turn. Shouldn't I be concerned about "angulation" at this point?

"Angulation"—tipping the upper body out over the outside ski (see Chapter 10, "Ice")—is not so important these days as it once was, thanks to stiffer boots and better skis. It is still important on ice, but for now, angulation—which used to be called the "comma position"—should not be exaggerated. It should just be a "happening" which results from the slope

27

itself and from the fact that the knees (particularly the downhill knee) are bending.

As you finish a turn and go into a traverse, it is as though you were walking along a street with one foot on the sidewalk and one foot in the gutter. Your whole body will obviously be tilted toward the gutter. This is all the angulation you need. As the slope gets steeper, the tilt is greater because the difference between the sidewalk and the gutter is greater.

How important is the "traverse position" really? Ski classes seem to spend hours and hours practicing traverses.

If you think about it you will realize that all turns after snowplow turns begin and end in the traverse position. But ski instructors, in trying to help people to begin and end their turns properly, have perhaps made too much of the traverse. Very good skiers, you will notice, try to avoid making long traverses. It appears that they are always either beginning or ending a turn. The traverse, as it has been taught in ski schools in the past, is one of those "poses" which *should* be avoided.

Sometimes traverses are necessary, such as when you are learning new turns. The traverse allows you time to get organized and think before you have to make a turn again. But it should look like nothing more than a "gorilla stance" as you ski across the hill. You should be slouched and facing the way you are going, with only as much angulation as the slope requires.

What about making turns from a traverse?

Try making your first turns from a very steep traverse—that's a traverse that is at only a slight angle to the fall line. As you get more confident, allow your traverses to get flatter and flatter. The motions are exactly the same as before: down and plant, up and forward, down and drive the knees (see Fig. 8).

As you begin to make turns from "flatter" traverses, you are going to have to turn further: now closer to 180 degrees than to 90 degrees. This means that you are going to have to unweight more, which means—that's right!—that you are going to have to sink down more to begin with. Be sure you allow yourself enough speed to carry you through the turn. Try putting two or three turns together as soon as you can.

I'm still stemming before I turn! How am I ever going to break that habit?

Stemming *is* a hard habit to break. At the risk of sounding like a stuck record, just let me say that it is impossible to emphasize the first down motion too much. I don't think I have *ever* seen a beginning parallel skier with too much down motion. As you sink down, try squeezing your knees together. This might help you resist the urge to stem.

If that doesn't work, try standing still and sinking very hard, pressing your ankles into your boots. Without changing your position at *all,* try to stem. If you are really low and really against the fronts of your boots, you can't! If you could, it was because you let yourself rise back up a little. You should begin your turns in this very low position.

Why can I turn better in one direction than I can in the other?

You know, you can analyze and understand all of the motions involved in hitting a backhand in tennis, but if you don't put the motions to-

1

FIGURE 8: *Parallel turn with up unweighting.* Your very first parallel turns across the fall line should be done with an *up* unweighting motion. Up unweighting is a little easier to feel and understand than are some of the other ways of making yourself momentarily light. The "lightness" resulting from an up motion seems to last longer than lightness caused by a quick *down* motion.

1. Here is the demonstrator in a comfortably high stance. Notice that "high" does not mean that he is standing so tall that his legs and body have straightened and stiffened. His right hand is about to come forward to make the pole plant.

2. He sinks down *and* plants the pole *in the same motion.* The pole plant "triggers" the *up,* which comes next. Note that the planting of the pole is as simple a move as reaching to shake hands—without fancy affectation.

Beginning parallel skiers should study this second figure carefully. Don't be afraid to exaggerate this down motion before the turn! Look at how he sinks forward into the boots. He does not just drop his fanny so that he weights the ski tails. He is standing right over the middle of the ski—exactly where he should be.

3. Now he comes up and *forward*—projecting his hips ahead—so that even at this highest point in his up motion he still has pressure against the *fronts* of the boots. He is unweighted at this point, but he has not "hopped" the skis off the snow. Remember that the lightness is ever so brief! If you come up too straight or stay up too long, you quickly become heavy again before you have a chance to complete the turn.

4. The second down motion begins *immediately.* The feet steer and the knees push *down* and in the direction of the turn. Can you see how this puts the skis on edge and applies pressure to the tips?

5. As he crosses the fall line the skier does not give up on the turn too quickly. See how he continues to use his legs to keep the skis turning so that he will come out of the turn in a fairly flat traverse and not gain too much speed.

6. Notice too how the upper body has remained square to the skis throughout

30

2

3

4

5

6

the entire turn. Because he can always see both hands and is facing ahead, he is always ready for the next turn. He can now plant his left pole, rise up and forward, and turn again.

Make one turn at a time and come to a stop if you are just beginning to make parallel turns. And don't feel that you necessarily have to look as elegant as the demonstrator in this illustration. Let your feet come apart a little to be more stable.

Try it: down . . . updown!

gether properly, you miss the ball. You are still missing the ball—at least in one direction. Making a turn in skiing is every bit as complex as hitting a tennis ball.

It is a very rare tennis player or golfer who can play equally well with either hand. Yet skiing makes the absurd demand that you turn equally well in both directions. Everyone has a good side and a bad side—even the very good skiers. It seems to have little to do with being right-handed or left-handed. Like all of us, you are going to have to work harder to perfect turns to your bad side.

What should I be doing with my hips?

Nothing! You have tremendous turning power in your body, centered mainly right at your hips. Golfers learn to use this power by rotating their hips as they drive a ball. In skiing, with a few exceptions (see Chapter 9, "Powder"), this is exactly what we try *not* to do. You can get great torque from rotating the hips—lots and lots of people unfortunately do just this—but if you do, you are unable to get any sort of "feel" for what your knees, feet, and edges are doing. This "feel" is vital when snow conditions are less than ideal. For this reason, all turning power should come from the knees and feet.

Again we are confronted with the question of women who, in some cases, have wider hips. I am never quite sure whether some women rotate their hips because they have more hip to rotate, whether they do so because they lack strength in their upper legs (which I usually doubt) and need extra torque, or whether in fact they simply *appear* to be rotating their hips more. Any slight hip motion is more apparent in a broad-hipped woman than in a man whose hips are narrower. To someone who may be watching very critically, the rotation may seem far more excessive and the problem far greater than it actually is. However, many of the gals I know who are excellent skiers have had to concentrate particularly hard on "blocking" their hips—seeing to it that the hips do not move—and on making the legs and feet work harder.

People who do not "complete" parallel turns properly with the knees and feet must compensate by rotating the hips. You can spot these people a mile away. The outside leg, the one that is about to become the downhill leg, is stiff as a board. As a result they rotate, and by the end of the turn, the upper body is faced back up the hill.

Is there any easy way to correct hip rotation?

Sure. Again, think of your hips as part of your upper body. If your upper body faces the way you are going, the hips should be facing the same way. Some people stiffen the downhill leg and rotate the hips because they are frightened by steepness. We can all sympathize with them, but all they are doing is compounding the problem. They "brace" with the down-hill leg as if hoping the mountain will go away. If the downhill leg is straight—always a "no-no" position in skiing—and the uphill leg is bent, you are leaning uphill, another skiing "no-no."

Bend the downhill leg so that you have a little natural angulation. Keep your belly button facing the way you are going: not uphill, not down-hill. If the belly button points ahead, the hips cannot rotate.

How can I keep from going so fast at the end of the turn?

The amount of turn you make in skiing, whether it's a snowplow turn or an advanced racing turn, is regulated by how much you bend the knee on the outside ski. If you bend the knee a lot, you put the ski on edge a lot and you turn a lot—sharply! If you only bend the knee a little,

FIGURE 9: *Wedeln.* Here we see *wedeln*—a skiing term derived from a German word meaning "waves." Wedeln is linked parallel turns which flow together with no abrupt edging of the skis to check the skier's speed. The technique is usually done on fairly smooth, reasonably gentle terrain. It can be done with up unweighting—as in this sequence—or with down unweighting (see Chapter 4). Sometimes the unweighting is so subtle that it hardly shows at all.

In this case wedeln consists of two basic motions:

A. A sinking motion which we refer to as "down" (#1, #4, #7, and #11). The down motion is preparation for unweighting. It is the beginning of the next turn and the completion of the previous turn all rolled into one. It is also the time when the legs and feet are doing the greatest amount of steering. The pole plant should always accompany the down.

B. The "lifting" or unweighting motion is called "up" (#2, #5, and #8). When the body stops extending (coming up), the skier is momentarily lighter, and the skis can be more easily steered as he sinks back down (#3–#4, #6–#7, and #9–#10).

To make smooth symmetrical tracks in the snow the skier must never hesitate, either during the "up" phase of the maneuver or during the "down" phase.

you only turn a little (unless you rotate the hips), and you build up too much speed.

"Stay with" your ski a little longer as you finish turning. "Complete" your turns by pushing harder and longer with the outside knee. This way you will come out of the turn into a flatter traverse and won't go charging into the next turn quite so fast.

Why does my downhill ski fall away from my uphill ski at the end of the turn?

This question is probably asked as often as any other by pretty good skiers. What you describe is called an "abstem" or "downstem." It is caused by not having the downhill ski on edge enough. If the knee does not bend as much as the arc of the turn requires, and the hips are rotated, and abstem is usually the result. The hip more or less controls what the tail of the ski does. If the hip turns, even a little, and the belly button faces even slightly uphill, you will lose the tail of the downhill ski.

In *linked* parallel turns, an abstem might be caused by "letting go" of the downhill ski a little too soon. Sometimes you begin to think about the next turn before you actually "complete" the previous one. It is right to be thinking ahead, but if you shift the weight to the uphill ski too early, the downhill ski will fall sloppily away.

All of this feels pretty good. When do I learn to wedel?

Right away, I hope. "Wedeln" is a marvelous mystery to novice skiers. Actually there is very little about it that is mysterious. It is really little more than linked parallel turns without any traverses. Anyone who can make good parallel turns can learn "wedeln" easily.

36

PARALLEL TURNS

It is absurdly simple if you can remember one thing: that the "down" motion that ends the very first turn turns right into the "up" motion for the next. In other words, instead of skiing in the pattern "Down-up-down-traverse, down-up-down-traverse," etc., you ski in the pattern "Down-up-down-UP-down-UP," etc. Start in the fall line again and give it a try (see Fig. 9).

That really fouled me up! What am I doing wrong?

Not much. In fact you are probably doing lots of things right. Don't try to make 40 turns in the space of 20 yards. Try to allow yourself enough time and space to establish a leisurely rhythm for yourself. Sometimes people will put in an extra little bouncy motion at first because they are not used to the "down-up-down-up" pattern. As you practice, try to make all of the motions coordinate smoothly with each other. This is of course the key to all good skiing.

Sometimes people will revert back to stemming as they first begin to wedel. Even more often they will abstem. This is okay at first, just so long as you know how to break these habits later on. Many get fouled up with their poles. As rhythm starts to play a more and more important role in your skiing, the pole plant becomes more and more important as a timing device. Plant your pole, as before, on the side to which you are about to turn. The pole is still planted on the *down;* not on the up.

Am I ready for expert slopes now?

Probably not yet. If you have come this far, though, you are probably ready to learn some of the techniques that will help you on much steeper slopes. But be sure that you are making good, solid parallel turns before you go on to anything new. It might not be a bad idea to go over some of the things in this chapter again.

3 Edgeset, Preturns, and Jet Turns

Once you get to the point where you can link good turns together with a fair amount of polish, it gets more and more difficult to recognize the component parts of an individual turn. If you eliminate the traverse, for example, each turn becomes inextricably related to the one that preceeded it as well as to the one that will come after it. This is as it should be.

But when we start to discuss something like "edgeset," are we talking about "edgeset" at the beginning of the *next* turn, or are we talking about "edgeset" at the completion of the *previous* one? Which came first, the chicken or the egg? It is one of those questions we could debate all we dlike—lots of ski technicians have, believe me!—but the ultimate answer doesn't really matter very much.

To keep things as simple as possible, let's equate "edgeset" with the "down" motion at the *beginning* of a parallel turn. (We could argue just as easily that it should be associated with the *second* "down.") If we permit ourselves to regard this "checking" motion—used on steeper terrain—as another "preparatory" move, we can conveniently lump together everything that happens before unweighting and call it all the "preturn."

The preturn does a lot more than slow us down as we go into the turn itself—although this *is* happily the case in the conventional "parallel turn with edgeset," which will be discussed first. As we get better and better at setting the edges to control speed, we will discover that the preturn sets us up for "jet" turns.

Before you get too excited—or upset—about that prospect, let me suggest that jet turns, in the technical sense at least, have nothing whatever to do with the flashy, fanny-dragging, tips-off-the-snow turns shown in ski movies and depicted on the covers of ski magazines. "Jetting" has been defined in various confusing terms. But what it all boils down to is that jetting is simply what happens to a skier's body and feet in reaction to an aggressive preturn.

Being able to "feel" and control your edges is the key to skiing steep slopes. I often feel ridiculous telling another skier to "feel the snow" with his edges when he is wearing rigid plastic boots and is standing on a moving board. It is almost like asking someone with novocaine in his feet to pick up a marble between his toes. Feeling your edges is a subtle skill that only time and mileage will develop. But learning and practicing preturns—making lots and lots of them in all kinds of conditions—will help you to become more and more conscious of what your legs, feet, and edges are doing in relation to the snow. In time, and with patience, the apparent anesthesia in your feet will begin to disappear. When this happens, whatever fear of clifflike ski slopes you may have will start to vanish too—although if you are human, it will never fade away completely.

How do I learn to make an edgeset?

First by learning how to "flatten" your skis, and how to put them on edge quickly. Stand on a moderately steep slope with your skis across the fall line. In order to keep your skis from sliding sideways, you will have to have your skis on edge. You probably don't need to think about it, but to place your skis on edge, you have to push your knees into the hill—uphill. Any intermediate skier will do this automatically while he is standing still.

Spread your arms apart, and plant one pole well above your feet and one below you. Sidestep up to your uphill pole—you will have to keep your skis on edge to do this. When you get to the pole, *release* your edges by gently pushing your knees away from the hill. This will cause the skis to flatten on the snow. Steadying yourself with your poles, let yourself slide sideways toward your downhill pole, keeping your weight centered more or less over the downhill ski. Before you get to the pole, stop the sideslip by pushing your knees back into the hill. As you push your knees in, you will notice that your angulation will naturally increase. This is an edgeset.

That's all there is to it?

That's all. Practice setting your edges *crisply*, so that the sideslip stops abruptly. Then try it without the support of your poles. Be sure that you are balanced properly on the skis—not too far back, not too far forward. If you are too far forward, you will start to ski ahead.

During the sideslipping phase be sure that the upper body faces the *direction of travel*—you are going *sideways* now, not forward. As you set the edges, making a down motion with your knees, plant your pole below you in the same motion. As you do, you should notice that the pole is planted almost directly in front of your body. Because you are facing sideways, this does *not* mean that you have planted the pole in front of your tips. Do lots of these.

EDGESET, PRETURNS, AND JET TURNS

Can I try it from a traverse?

That's the next step (look at Fig. 10). First try to incorporate edgeset and the "uphill christie" to make what some technicians have appropriately called a "hockey stop." From a fairly high traversing "gorilla stance," allow yourself a bit of speed, flatten your edges, let your skis slip a bit, then sink—abruptly pushing your knees into the hill. You should make a quick uphill christie to a stop. Your tips will have climbed back up the hill.

Try it a second time, only now try not to let your upper body turn with the skis, as you learned in the uphill christie (turn back to the illustration of the uphill christie, Fig. 5, if you like), but keep your body facing in the direction of the original traverse while your *feet* and *skis* turn uphill (#3–#4 in Fig. 10). As you sink and come to a stop, plant your pole to steady yourself. Are you facing the pole?

Should I feel the tails of my skis falling away downhill?

Yes, you might. This is why this maneuver has sometimes been called "heel thrust." One well-known ski writer has even gone so far as to say, "Weight primarily the tails of your skis as you begin pivoting" into the preturn.[1] This can set a dangerous precedent by getting you into the habit of sitting back too much. I personally would prefer to have you thinking about your tips rather than about your heels and your tails, but this approach does help some people who are having trouble learning preturns.

Some instructors have had success teaching edgeset by encouraging people to abstem on purpose (see the question about abstem in Chapter 2).

[1] Georges Joubert, *Teach Yourself to Ski* (Aspen, Colo.: Aspen Ski Masters, 1970), p. 87.

FIGURE 10: *Edgeset.* Making an effective "preturn" with edgeset is a skill which every aspiring expert skier must develop. It involves a great deal more than being able to check your speed before a turn. Notice how the skis in this illustration change direction, but the upper body does not. In this particular instance the demonstrator made an edgeset to a stop. The upper body, nonetheless, faces the way the skis would be *about* to go if this preturn were to develop into a turn across the fall line. (See Fig. 12, the jet turn, which looks like a continuation of this maneuver.)

1. The demonstrator is skiing in a fairly steep traverse. He is also going pretty fast. The skis are on edge.

2. Here we can see the skis begin to flatten slightly. In another foot or so they will begin to skid. The left hand is bringing the pole forward and preparing for the pole plant.

3. Now the skis have been pivoted and the tips steered uphill. See how the skier's weight is over the center of the skis? He is neither too far back nor too far forward. He wants to use the *whole* length of the skis to his advantage—not just a portion of them. The hand comes forward to make the pole plant as the knees drive ahead to put the skis back on edge and stop the skidding action.

4. Here the edges have been set. The skier's feet have come to an abrupt stop. It is almost as if he has tripped himself—on purpose, of course. The upper body, on the other hand, still has momentum and wants to continue forward as you can see. The planted pole—which he now faces—helps to prevent him from falling over. This momentum in the upper body can later be used to assist in the turn.

Practice this move, but be careful that you don't initiate your preturn by moving the hips. Remember: the hips should be considered part of the upper body. See how they, like the shoulders, have not rotated as the skis change direction.

By abstemming the downhill ski, people can gradually be taught to make *both* skis do the same thing to make a parallel preturn.[2] This is taking a bad habit and turning it into something good. It certainly seems to be a means to a justifiable end. It may work for you. Try it.

I see. So a "preturn" is sort of an uphill christie but without coming to a stop, right?

Right—with your upper body facing the direction of travel, not necessarily the way the skis are pointing. In the preturn, because your *skis* are at an angle to the direction of travel, you are braking. It is obviously not your intention to ski back up the hill. If you preturn with your skis—allowing your upper body to face up the hill—you are doing what is called a "wind-up" for the turn. This is a superfluous motion that can lead to even worse problems.

How do I use this preturn in my skiing?

Substitute it for the initial "down" motion in the conventional parallel turn. What you will be doing is called, oddly enough, a "parallel turn with edgeset" or a "parallel turn with a check." Preturn with a sharp edgeset and pole plant to slow yourself, come up and forward, and than back down, completing the turn in the normal way. Rise up slightly before the next turn so that you can go back down again.

The preturn has often been described as establishing a "platform" (#4 in Fig. 10) from which you can make your "up" unweighting motion—an appropriate description. Remember to be well forward as you come up from the platform.

[2] Abraham, pp. 27–29.

EDGESET, PRETURNS, AND JET TURNS

None of this is really new.
In what way is a jet turn different?

A lot has been written and said lately about jet turns. Really it is not all that different from the parallel turn with edgeset. The emphasis is just shifted a little. The jet turn uses the very steep pitch of a slope to aid in the turn. As any slope gets steeper, it is actually easier to unweight and change direction because you have gravity helping you more.

When you make a preturn at some speed on a steep slope, you are "checking" or inhibiting your downhill progress. Your feet may feel like they want to stop, but the upper body wants to keep on going. We have all had the embarrassing experience of coming to a stop too suddenly and fall- ing over. The jet turn, in many ways, is like intentionally tripping your- self. If you are ready for it, you can resist the urge to fall downhill on your face as your feet slow down. If you have your balance, the deceleration will make you feel like you are being squashed—compressed—by a giant hand. It is the same sensation you feel when you are riding in an elevator that stops suddenly.

You mean that gravity takes care of the first
down motion?

Sort of. It's a little like compressing a spring or holding a beach ball under water. If you let the spring or the beach ball go, it will fly up. In ski- ing this release of downward pressure is called "rebound." Rebound is a natural reaction—a kind of passive unweighting. If you set your edges so hard that your body is compressed (#1 in Fig. 11), and then relax your legs, your skis will "jet"—*rebounding* off the edge of the downhill (inside) ski, and pivoting toward the fall line as you shift weight to the outside ski (#2). Sounds pretty complicated, doesn't it?

45

FIGURE 11: *Rebound.* "Rebound" is an important kind of unweighting. It is another one of those passive "happenings" which result from something else. But rebound cannot work for you until you have learned how to make an aggressive edgeset! You will get only as much rebound from an edgeset as you put *ummph* into it.

Here is a good one:

1. The deceleration from this edgeset is so abrupt that the pompom on the skier's hat has flopped forward out of view. Notice how violently he has edged the skis. Notice also how the upper body has "anticipated." It faces the way the skier is *about* to turn—not toward the tips of the skis. The planted pole (which the skier faces) helps to stabilize the upper body at this point.

Two things are happening in this first figure. First, the skis are being forced into "reverse camber." This means that they are very much like a compressed leaf spring. Second, the body is being squashed by the additional G-forces caused by the sudden slowing down.

2. I can assure you that the demonstrator has *not* made an active up motion. He has gotten into this second position as a result of several things (all of which happen in less than an instant):

(a) The compressed skis—still operating like a leaf spring—recoil and assume their original shape. They also want to accelerate ahead—or "jet."

(b) The muscles in the body react to the sudden stop just the way they would in someone riding in an elevator which comes to a jerky halt. Human muscles are most comfortable when the body is standing erect. They "rebound," returning the body to a more normal position.

(c) The skis (and the lower body) want to align themselves with the upper body, which has *anticipated* the turn (see Chapter 4).

(d) The feet have helped to pivot the skis toward the fall line.

If all of this quasi-physics seems like too much for your mind to grasp all at once (which wouldn't surprise me a bit), squint your eyes at the illustration and try to imagine what this turn *feels* like.

If you still can get no feeling for this maneuver I would be willing to bet that you still have never experienced what it is like to make a really severe edgeset. Go out and practice some more.

46

It sure does. You mean I don't have to unweight at all?

Try to *feel* it more and intellectualize it less. Things will happen so fast that you will not have time to think them through. First try making a turn at pretty good speed on a fairly steep slope. "Hit" your edges hard as you make the preturn. You slow down, but you don't come to a stop. You feel the compression, the pole is planted, and the upper body is faced ahead. Now *actively* come up and forward. You will probably get all sorts of lift because you are assisting the rebound by coming up yourself. In fact the tails of the skis may actually come right off the snow. This is *not* a "jet" turn.

In your *next* turn, allow yourself even more speed, and hit your edges even harder as you make your pole plant (#3-#4 in Fig. 12), then *relax* your legs—don't come up even though it seems to be the thing to do at this point—and let the skis "jet." You will feel as though your whole body wants to recoil from the compression. Don't fight it (#5). Shift your weight to the outside ski and pivot the skis to the fall line (#6). This is a jet turn.

Why do I lose my balance just as my feet get to the fall line?

For the same reason that you lost your balance in learning a parallel turn when you did not come up and *forward*. Try to stay with your feet. Since in the jet turn you don't come *up* and forward, you are going to have to be ready for the jetting effect in a slightly different way. When your feet slow down as a result of the edgeset, *let* your upper body continue ahead (#4 in Fig. 12). (You won't fall downhill, remember, because you are not really going to come to a stop.) When the jetting "happens," you won't get caught behind your feet as the skis start to

48

accelerate. Some very good skiers say they have the feeling that the upper body is "pulling" the skis into the fall line.

How can I keep my skis from accelerating in the fall line?

Lots of people ask this question. You *can't* keep your skis from accelerating when they are pointing right down the hill! There is no such thing as a "decelerating turn" across the fall line (unless you snowplow). All parallel turns have some acceleration, but this shouldn't frighten you. By now you know how to slow down either before or after the fall line.

On very steep slopes you obviously want to stay in the fall line for as brief a time as possible. Remember that all unweighting—either active or passive—only helps you to get *to* the fall line. It will not finish any turn for you. You must still use your legs and feet to torque you through the later phases of the turn.

What is "shortswing"? Is it different from wedeln?

"Shortswing," sometimes called "check wedeln," is just linked parallel turns with edgeset. Each "down" is an edgeset. The amount of edgeset you use is determined by the steepness of the hill and by how fast you want to be going. In wedeln there is no edgeset *per se*, although each turn may be "completed" enough to slow you down. Both shortswing and wedeln involve an active up-unweighting motion. Sometimes it is difficult or even impossible to see the difference between the two. Fine distinctions like this should be left to the nitpickers anyway.

Linked jet turns—an advanced form of shortswing reserved for perilously steep terrain—is not that different either (see Fig. 13). The weighting of the skis is still the same—"outside ski to outside ski." Each apparent "down" is still a checking preturn (#2, #6, #9), but there is

49

FIGURE 12: *The jet turn.* Jetting—like rebound—is a modern ski's natural reaction to a severe edgeset. If a skidding ski is suddenly placed on edge to stop its skid, the ski will accelerate almost as if it were ricocheting off the snow. If a skier stands *precisely* over the middle of the ski he may only get rebound—which means no acceleration. If he stands very slightly back on the ski he will get both rebound and jetting. A very good skier tries never to let a ski jet by accident. But he may intentionally use jetting to help him pivot the skis toward the fall line.

1. A jet turn requires a certain amount of speed. Here we see the demonstrator approaching the turn fairly fast.

2. He begins his preturn as his left hand prepares for the pole plant.

3–4. The flattened skis skid (or carve, depending on the terrain and the texture of the snow) through the checking preturn.

5. Here the skis are violently placed on edge, stopping the sideways skid and causing the feet to decelerate and then shoot ahead. The upper body continues forward in the original direction of travel. As the skis jet following the edgeset the skier will quickly pivot the skis and relax his legs so that the skis will seek the fall line.

6. Notice how the skier is more extended (in a higher stance) here as a result of the rebound.

50

7–8. Now the knees are directed away from the fall line again as the demonstrator's attention focuses on the next preturn.

The jet turn is probably the most misunderstood maneuver in all of skiing. It involves little more than taking advantage of the natural forces of acceleration and deceleration which surround the edgeset. Many good skiers make jet turns without realizing it. Study this sequence again and see that at no time is the skier in a position of serious imbalance. The *extreme* sit-back position extolled by some skiing publications has nothing whatever to do with true jet turns.

FIGURE 13: *Linked jet turns.* "Shortswing" performed by a good skier who really knows how to set an edge may consist of little more than a series of jet turns. This sequence was taken on *very* hard snow near the top of the Nose Dive at Stowe, after the run had been groomed by machinery and the moguls taken out. The skier's facial expression tells you something about how hard he is concentrating on setting his edges and controlling his speed. Notice how much the legs must work to roll the skis up on edge.

1. Study this figure of the demonstrator planting his pole. It is nearly mirrored in #6 and again in #9. Now look quickly at all of the others. Do you see how the upper body and hips in all of the figures are pointing in basically the same direction—down the fall line? This is always either the direction the skier is going or the way he is *about* to go.

2. Here we see the first edgeset . . .

3. . . . . and here we see the "pivoted rebound" which results from that edgeset.

4. The skier passes through the fall line . . .

5. . . . and quickly *completes* the turn to counteract the acceleration he feels as a result of having crossed the fall line.

6. The completion of one turn is the preturn for the next. The edges are set a second time.

7. Now we can see a very clear illustration of how the skis have jetted. See how the skier's feet seem to have shot ahead? He is *not* off balance—partly because he is stabilized by the pole, but mostly because he is projecting his upper body in the direction of the turn and is ready to steer the skis back across the fall line again.

8. Here he is still perfectly balanced over the middle of the skis as the second turn is completed.

9. The edges start to bite for the third time—perhaps not quite as effectively this time. (See the spray of snow?)

10. But now the edges have taken hold and the skidding has stopped . . .

11. . . . . and rebound happens again.

1 2 3 4 5 6 7 8 9 10 11

53

no active "up" (#3-#4, #6-#7, #10-#11). Instead the skier is repeatedly taking advantage of rebound and jetting. If you already wedel and can understand the theory of jetting, you can learn to make linked jet turns fairly quickly.

What happens to the upper body and hips when turns are linked together so closely?

That's an astute question. The immediate temptation is to answer by saying, "Nothing." The upper body *is* very quiet. There certainly should be no rotation or counter-rotation. If you look closely you will see that the upper body and hips are always facing right down the fall line. The pole plant is right in front of your torso. The feet and legs seem to twist back and forth beneath the upper body, which *seems* to be doing nothing. But notice how the upper body always seems to be in a position awaiting—*anticipating*—the next turn. This expectant posture is precisely what "anticipation" is all about—as we shall see.

What goals should I be setting for myself now?

Before you go on to anything new, you might spend some time thinking about what is called "total motion." Camouflage and disguise individual motions within the totality of your skiing. Your whole body wants to be in motion all the time. As Horst Abraham has said, "Continuous motion does not imply that one motion has to last throughout the entire maneuver, but rather that the body is never *locked* in any position, and one motion follows smoothly into another."[3] Work at perfecting the turns you already have learned, by making them smoother.

[3] Abraham, p. 7.

54

4 Anticipation and Other Ways to Unweight

Racers are the only great innovators in ski technique—not ski instructors, not expert skiers. Racers are forever looking for faster, better, more efficient ways of doing things on the snow because they have to ski on the brink of disaster all the time. Anyone who doesn't ski all-out will be beaten, because somebody else will. The good technicians and good instructors watch the good racers to see what they are doing that is different, and take from them what they can use themselves.

Unfortunately this happens much too slowly. Ski-school methods are sometimes as much as five years behind the top racers. This is not to suggest that a ski school's objective should be to produce racers. Few skiers are after a spot on an Olympic team; many don't even necessarily want to emulate what the racers are doing. Be that as it may, there is a lot to be learned from the topflight racers. For instance, one of the most striking things about the competitors in the past few years—aside from the appallingly aggressive speeds they ski at—is that only occasionally do they unweight in the conventional way, with "down-up."

All of us, whether we are old racers, ski-schooled, or self-taught, are more or less conditioned to come "up and forward" to unweight. This certainly is the easiest and, in many situations, the best way to do it. But being able to unweight in only one way can be a handicap if you want to be a very good skier. It is like being a basketball player with only one shot, or a poet who insists on writing only in blank verse. You can "make it" for a while with only one "thing," but in time you cannot compete with others who are more flexible.

Even the jet turn is really little more than a sophistication of the parallel turn with edgeset and "up" motion—although the up motion is not nearly so self-conscious as in the conventional parallel turn. Jet turns are useful and exciting, but they are not the ultimate in ski technique.

There *are* other ways to unweight. Instead of coming up, for instance, it is possible to unweight by going down. It is also possible to turn without unweighting at all. It is possible, as has been suggested in the last chapter, to turn by twisting the upper body and projecting it in the direction of the turn. This, as you must know by now, is called "anticipation."

To understand anticipation a little better, let's amend one of the two basic principles suggested in Chapter 1. Instead of saying, "Keep your upper body facing the way you are going," let's say, "Keep your upper body facing the way you are going—or are *about* to go." Anticipation—facing the upper body the way you are about to go—is another "preparatory" motion, like the preturn. Like many skiing maneuvers, it can be done "pure"—without edgeset—or it can be done in combination with other things, like jetting.

Anticipation was recognized and developed, not to take the place of conventional ski-school turns, but to reinforce and improve upon them. It is a way of skiing a lot more smoothly and with a lot less effort. Instead of having to unweight with a relatively jerky up motion, we can unweight laterally—or sideways.

56

ANTICIPATION AND OTHER WAYS TO UNWEIGHT

Is that why everyone says that anticipation is so frightening?

There is nothing any more frightening about anticipation than there is about something like counter-rotation. Very good skiers, as well as racers, have been using it for years without realizing it. Nobody bothered to call it anything. I am amused when an older very good skier—sometimes a professional—maintains that anticipation is a lot of hogwash but can be seen using it constantly.

Georges Joubert, the great French technician, was the first to recognize how the anticipated upper body helped the skis to turn. I don't know where the public got the idea that is was something scary or that it was some new gimmick to get people to come to ski school. In its purest form, it *is* an almost entirely different way of turning. This may be what seems frightening about it.

What's the best preparation for learning anticipation?

Willingness to try something new is more important than anything else. There *are* a few things you could be doing with your hands that might help:

1. Remember how it helped your body position when you learned to plant your pole farther ahead as you gained speed? Now, as the slope gets steeper, you will also find it helpful to reach farther *downhill* as you plant your pole. Later this will make it easier to get your upper body going in the direction of the turn.

2. On those very steep places where you worry about getting down in one piece, it is easy to forget about being able to see both hands. Get them out in front of you again where you can see them and where they can do you some good! I had a racing coach who once said, "If you can get your hands through the slalom gate first, the rest of you has to follow."

This is an oversimplification, of course, and he knew it. But it does help to build confidence by getting your upper body into a good aggressive "attack" position.

3. Try for "total motion" in your hands as well as in the rest of you. Concentrate on keeping your outside hand in motion. *Reach* for the next turn as you complete the previous one. If you do, not only will your hand never disappear from the field of vision, but your rhythm will improve as you make linked turns.

Don't you use the outside hand to help you make an anticipation turn?

If you vigorously swing your outside arm around to assist you in the turn, you are using old-fashioned upper-body rotation à la Emile Alais, a Frenchman who made that technique famous. As far as I am concerned, rotation is not so bad as long as it is not overdone. The upper body should rotate only as fast as the skis turn. If your trunk turns faster, it will face back up the hill at the end of each turn.

Too many skiers are confused about the difference between anticipation and the natural "square" stance so many good skiers are using today. In anticipation the outside hand does follow through with the body, but it does not supply any turning power. The body rotates—with the turning skis—only *after* the turn has been started by anticipation.

Is there any way I can feel anticipation work while I am standing still?

You can use a small mogul to help you. Stand with your feet right on the very crest of a bump (see Fig. 14) Your skis should be across the fall line. The tips and tails will be off the snow. You want to be just teetering.

58

FIGURE 14: *Anticipation—standing still.* The human body is uncomfortable when it is twisted out of its normal stance. The muscles and skeletal system work to bring themselves back into a more comfortable aligned position. You can put this natural body alignment to work for you in your skiing. Feel it first while you are standing on the crest of a bump.

Turn and look right down the fall line. Reach down and plant your downhill pole directly below your feet. Now reach a little farther below your feet with your pole. Now a little farther, until you feel that you are about to fall on your face. Now let your skis slide ahead a little. Even if you fight it, you will make a turn toward the fall line as you ski off the bump.

Why?

You twisted your upper body to face downhill, for one thing—not ahead. By twisting this way, and starting to lean downhill—with the help of the exaggerated pole plant—the feet and skis naturally wanted to align themselves with the upper body as soon as you started to slide.[1]

The fact that you were teetering on the bump helped too. Only the midsections of your skis were in contact with the snow. As a result, there was very little frictional resistance to your skis turning. They could come around very easily with the help of anticipation.

How does anticipation work when I am in motion?

The same way it does when you are standing still. It's like taking a popsicle stick and twisting it with your fingers, turning one end in one direction and the other end the opposite way. If you let go of one end, the stick will snap back to its original flat shape—assuming that you haven't broken it.

Think of the body as a popsicle stick. If you are moving across the slope on skis, with your knees into the hill (which puts your skis on their uphill edges), and you turn your upper body downhill, you have twisted both ends of your body in opposite directions (see #1 in Fig. 15). If you

[1] Abraham, p. 3.

60

FIGURE 15: *Anticipation on smooth terrain—the human popsicle stick.* To really understand what is going on in this illustration, try an experiment. Hold your right arm straight out in front of you, palm up. With your left hand, twist your right hand and wrist clockwise until it almost hurts. This is basically what is happening in #1. The body is being wound in opposite directions.

Now let go of your right hand. See it snap back into its original position? This same thing is taking place in #2, #3, and #4. The edge release in #2 permits the body to unwind itself. "Body alignment" is an expression frequently used to describe what happens as a result of anticipation.

then release your edges, by pushing your knees the way the upper body already faces, the lower body and skis will seek the line the shoulders have just established, and the turn is well under way.

So what's so hard about anticipation?

Nothing. It's easy. The hardest thing for some people is letting it work! It is one thing to understand it in your head, and another thing to make your legs and feet understand it too. Some never get the feel of anticipation at all because they are stuck in an up-motion rut. They try, but just at the point when alignment is about to happen all by itself, they chicken out and make an up motion. Up motion can get so ingrained that learning something new is like trying to stop a reflex action. Exaggerate anticipation, especially if you are trying to learn it on a very flat slope—and *wait* a split-second longer for the anticipation to work for you.

On very steep slopes it is hard psychologically to twist and drop your upper body out into space. But you won't fall off the side of the mountain, I promise. In fact you will be stunned at how fast the skis will whip around with the help of anticipation.

Why do I suddenly seem to be losing sight of my outside hand?

You are probably concentrating so hard on the preparatory phases of the turn that you are forgetting that you must finish it as well. Pretend that every time you make a turn, you are going to pass through an imaginary doorway below you. As you approach the door, turn and face it. You reach out with the downhill hand and turn the doorknob—extending your arm to plant your pole. Your skis will start to pivot as the edges are released.

Instead of opening the door in the normal way—by pushing it open

62

with the hand that is on the doorknob—reach around with your *other* hand to push the door open. Then as your skis turn, your outside hand will follow through, and will stay where you can see it.

Sometimes I lose sight of my hand because it is up too high!

An outside hand that is *much* higher than the inside hand is symptomatic of a more serious problem: you are leaning to the inside of the turn too much and may come out of it leaning uphill. Not only is this bad in itself, but it will make getting into the next turn terribly difficult.

As you anticipate with your upper body you should still see your outside hand out of the corner of your eye. It should be out there somewhere beside your knees. Because in this type of turn you are letting yourself lean into the turn to help *initiate* the pivoting of the skis, it is very easy to forget about angulation at the end. If you lean inside for too long, the hand flies up. As you push the door open with your outside hand, push the hand *down* as well. This will help to ensure that most of the weight is on the outside ski, because you will be forced to lean that way.

Do you lean on the pole when you "turn the doorknob"?

It sometimes looks that way when you watch others doing it. But you should never be using your pole as a crutch. If you do, you will *really* be leaning uphill at the end of the turn.

Think of the pole as a balancing point that stabilizes the upper body, but not as a pivot point. Use it to steady you as you project your body out

63

SKI WITH THE BIG BOYS

and away from the mountain and in the direction of the turn. Rather than lean on it, let the pole, and your momentum past it, gently push your body *away* from the spot where the pole was planted so that you tip slightly and naturally away from the turn.

How do I get ready for the next turn?

What happens in the anticipation turn is that the upper body takes a short cut. The feet, in the meantime, go around the long way to make the arc of the turn. The pole helps you to balance yourself as your feet catch up to your upper body. As your feet catch up, you should have some natural angulation.

As the outside hand comes around—nice and low, remember—let it continue forward to reach for the next doorknob. This should increase your angulation still more as you reach well down the hill. This exaggerated angulation, as you face down the fall line, is—not so miraculously—anticipation for the next turn.

Can anticipation be combined with other things?

You bet it can! If you check some of the earlier illustrations in this book, you will see anticipation all over the place. In fact, only rarely do you see a skier making a "pure" anticipation turn. He may anticipate and come "up" too—depending on the situation. Nothing wrong with that!

He might anticipate like mad during an edgeset for a jet turn (see Fig. 18 in the next chapter), and use a combination of anticipation and rebound to carry him through the turn. I have even seen people use anticipation in stem christies. It is an invaluable move in bumps, and a vital part of the "squatty-body" turn which will come later.

64

ANTICIPATION AND OTHER WAYS TO UNWEIGHT

Why would anyone want to use anticipation instead of "down-up"?

If you are still a skeptic, you have obviously still never felt what it is like to make an anticipation turn. In fact, you have probably never really watched a very good skier virtually oozing down a slope making linked turns with anticipation and no apparent up motion at all. That has got to be one of the prettiest sights in all of sport—"poetry in motion."

As you get older, perhaps—or just more tired—you will begin to look for more effortless ways to turn your skis. Maybe then you will be convinced. Until then I can only repeat a now famous quotation: "Try it. You'll like it!"

Why does it seem easier to make an anticipation turn on a steeper slope?

It is always *physically* harder to change direction on a flatter slope than it is to turn on a steeper one. You have to unweight more where it is flat. In the conventional parallel turn you have to put added effort in your "up."

Anticipation—like rebound—is just another way of unweighting. Exaggerate it as much as you can on the flat, and let yourself ski a little faster if possible. Generally, as you go faster, your need to unweight is diminished. Sometimes, where it is too flat, anticipation won't work at all. If it doesn't, just unweight the old way.

Is it possible to anticipate too much?

It is just like anything else—you *can* go overboard, going to all sorts of awkward, pretentious, and contorted extremes. Other skiers—if this is

65

important to you—will be watching for finesse and discriminating exactness in your skiing, very much the way real *aficionados* of the bullfights will watch a matador. In their sophisticated pettiness they will pick out little mistakes. But they are really passing judgment on style.

One generally agreed-upon measurement of anticipation has to do with the outside hand. If the hand passes across the skis before the turn begins, some will say that this is too much anticipation. Others will argue that this is really rotation. At this point you should not be concerned with this sort of hairsplitting. When you are first learning anticipation, don't worry too much about overdoing things. Refinement can come later.

What other ways of unweighting are there?

We have already talked about rebound and jetting as a kind of passive unweighting. The terrain itself can be helpful in unweighting too—in fact, this is what the next chapter is about.

The most common way to unweight actively without an up motion—and without the help of steepness or a bump—is "down unweighting." Many skiers do this naturally without being taught. When we were learning how to do an uphill christie, we were actually down unweighting.

How does down unweighting work?

If you were to go back to the bathroom scale again, you would see that you can unweight by standing in a relatively high position and suddenly dropping to a lower one. All that happens is that you lower your center of gravity so quickly that you make yourself lighter for an instant.

This is a very short-lived lightness and not recommended for beginning parallel skiers who are trying to make turns from one traverse to another at fairly slow speeds. A more advanced skier can turn by dropping from a natural "gorilla stance" into an angulated position while he sharply puts his skis on edge.[2]

When should I down-unweight?

Down unweighting seems to be most effective at high speed, on relatively flat terrain, when the snow is particularly slippery—even icy (see Fig. 29 in Chapter 10). In fact, in linked turns on frozen granular snow, if you can be dropping and edging all in the same motion *without* having to make an up, you will feel more secure. Many skiers feel very confident skiing on ice this way.

I probably don't need to point out that you cannot keep dropping and edging forever. You can go down only so far. After each turn you must, of course, rise up a little to be ready for the next. The pattern becomes "DOWN, easy up, DOWN, easy up, DOWN, easy up," etc.

Is there any way to turn without unweighting?

Certainly. If you press your knees forward and lean the way you want to go, the skis will turn. This is called "banking." It is a little bit tricky and will be discussed in another chapter. In some situations you can turn simply by swiveling your feet. We'll see about that too.

You can make your skis turn in still another way. Point your skis straight down the fall line on a gentle slope and get into a low tucked position. As you ski, stand up *very* slowly—gradually extending your whole body. As you extend, feel yourself pushing down with the big toe on your left foot. This will put that ski on edge and apply pressure to the tip. As long as you can extend, you can apply pressure to that big toe. You will

---

[2] This description of "down unweighting" comes from Abraham, p. 7.

FIGURE 16: *Down weighting and up weighting.* Most good skiers, like effective baseball pitchers, "mix things up" when they ski for themselves. In other words, they use the various ways of weighting and unweighting in different combinations. Very rarely, for instance, will we see someone performing shortswing using nothing but pure up unweighting. Down unweighting or rebound or up *weighting* will probably sneak into the act somehow.

(Continued next page)

Here we see a clear example of a turn which is made without any unweighting at all. The demonstrator is applying pressure and turning force to the skis by doing two entirely different things—both in the same turn.

1. In #1–#6 he is "down weighting," or *flexing*. By *gradually* dropping from a high stance (#1) to a much lower stance (#6) and driving his knees in the direction of the turn, he is able to maintain a constant pressure against the edged skis. That is, he is pushing *down* against them. (This is not down *un*weighting because he is not dropping very suddenly.) The skis oblige, when this kind of pressure is applied, by changing direction and carving the turn.

2. By #6 he has reached a point where he can go no lower without sitting back, or much farther forward because the boots won't give any more. But the turn is not completed yet. So he begins to move his body in the opposite direction and begins to *extend* again.

This second phase of the turn involves *up* weighting. As long as he can keep extending, he can maintain downward pressure against the edge—even though he appears to be coming up. Once he runs out of body extension (when he has reached his full height) he must either stop turning, or continue the turn (he could start a new one for that matter) by going back down again!

Sound confusing? Study the photos again.

find that you can sque-e-e-e-e-eze out a wide turn to the right. This is called "up *weighting.*"

That's very interesting, but does up weighting have any practical application?

You better believe it does! The "gorilla stance" makes it easy for you to absorb or "suck up" bumps, by breaking at all joints. When you ski over a particularly large bump, the bump will compress you—if you let it—into a tuck (recall Chapter 1). But then, if the bump is steep, the bottom drops out from under you.

The *only* way to keep your skis on the snow at this point is to up-weight—by pushing both feet back down, causing your whole body to extend. Some people call this "up-down-up," although that is not an entirely accurate description.

Being able to extend *and* turn in the same motion is clearly a useful procedure when the snow suddenly drops away beneath you. Usually up weighting in the bumps is preceded by anticipation and a preturn with rebound. Up weighting is a worthwhile thing to work on before committing your body to the *real* big bumps. And down weighting and up weighting can be used in combination (see Fig. 16).

You mean I have to master all these kinds of weighting and unweighting before I can become a "very good skier"?

Not long ago a lady came to me and said, "I want you to teach my friend to ski. I learned at Vail over Christmas." I had no doubts that she *had* learned a lot at Vail, but I tried not to laugh. One of the many, many things that makes skiing as fascinating as a lot of other complicated things is that the more you learn about it, the more you realize how much there is that you *don't* know. *All* of us are learning to ski. There is no one who "knows how." As soon as we think that we are getting to the point where we know everything, someone will come along with something new.

But almost always, thankfully, this "something new" turns out to be a variation on a theme we are already familiar with. Try to think of things like anticipation, down weighting, and down unweighting as modifications of what you are already doing well, not as something that you have to learn from scratch.

If you don't use at least some of the things suggested in this chapter, you are—unconsciously perhaps—confining yourself to just skiing advanced-intermediate slopes on near-perfect snow conditions. Try not to be intimidated by something new, or discouraged by what you haven't perfected yet. If you are any kind of serious skier at all, you already know that when skiing—and the mountains you do it on—cease to be humiliating, at least once in a while, you will rapidly lose interest in it.

———

5 *Bumps*

You're not a virtuoso yet. All it will take is a field of small bumps to remind you of that. Remember this scene?

It was a nice day . . . sunny . . . good snow . . . you were really quite
impressed with yourself, right? . . . the feet were parallel, but not *too* close
together . . . anticipation . . . a little jetting here and there . . . relaxed . . .
both hands in sight . . . you came around a bend in the trail (into the
shade, maybe?) . . . not too fast . . . everything under control . . . then
there was that little patch of bumps . . . no sweat . . . just a little traverse
to start things off. Right?

Suddenly you lost all confidence and started bouncing. And once you
started bouncing, you could never make up your mind to make a turn.
You were even a little scared, so you kept hesitating. The woods got closer
and closer. You had to make a turn! So you made a lousy one—a little off
balance. Then you bounced back to the other side, made another bad turn,

73

and were barely able to stay under control. You *probably* never even fell. But you didn't really *ski* either. The skis and the bumps were taking *you* for a ride.

And then it was over, thank God! A check, and you were in control of things again . . . anticipation . . . a little jetting here and there . . . and you continued, hoping no one had noticed what happened in the mogul field.

This experience—which we have all shared at one time or another—can mark a turning point in the career of skier. You can do one of two things at this point: you can quietly resolve not to go down that way again and go off seeking other smoother slopes, or you can decide to go up again and do better next time. All very good skiers made the second choice somewhere along the line. You *can* do better, and you *should* try.

All of those moves which you struggled so hard to learn seem to disintegrate when you get into the bumps. This discovery is sometimes hard to take. But don't be discouraged. You should have all of the fundamentals used in skiing bumps pretty much under control by now. You just need to make some minor adjustments. Maybe this is a good time to set down a new set of principles for skiing bumps.

1. *Never pose!* Avoid *any* static position—particularly the traverse. Always try to keep your skis *turning* in the bumps. A set of moguls might force you into a rhythm that you *must* accept—one that you may not be used to. Be ready, with your hands ahead and your weight on the balls of your feet.

2. *Stay loose.* Stay in the "gorilla stance." Now you are going to *have* to believe in it. Bumps are unforgiving. When you make a mistake on a smooth slope, you usually have time and room to recover. Not so in the bumps. Fortunately, with the help of that "natural athletic stance," you can "erase" small bumps by retracting your legs and folding and unfolding your body as you ski over them.[1]

[1] Joubert, p. 93

3. *Look and think ahead.* For the first time you are limited in your choice of route. Skiing bumps is a little like skiing slalom—the most intellectual of all skiing events. Somebody once said, "A good slalom skier is skiing in one gate, looking at the next, and thinking about the one after that." Be sure to keep your head up and watch how the rhythm—or lack of it—is developing ahead.

How well do conventional parallel turns work in the bumps?

Very well, as long as you are going slowly (see Fig. 17). You approach the bump, sink down and plant the pole (#1), and then come "up" (#2). The "up" more or less carries you over the top of the bump, where you shift your weight and drive your knees in the direction of the turn (#3). You may find that the tails actually lift off the snow (#2)—without your trying to make them—as you go over the top of the bump.

Some skiers take advantage of this bonus "lift" by "hopping" the tails over the crest of the bump before completing the turn. (Where I ski, this is called the "Stowe hop" because it is used so much.) It is a steady and secure way to ski in small bumps.

But?

But there are better ways besides the most conventional one. You are again limiting yourself severely if you only use this technique. Mr. Joubert says it better than I can:

"You do not dare to ski fast because you feel yourself catapulted into the air. Would you be a down-up motion specialist? At slow speeds a handsome up motion will bring you just to the top of the bump and result in a

FIGURE 17: *Conventional parallel turn on a bump.* Too much unweighting may cause you to lose contact with the snow. But this is not always bad. Skiing over a bump will give you a "lift." This is one kind of "terrain unweighting." If you combine terrain unweighting with an active up motion, you may find that the tails of the skis actually come off the snow. This is sound technique for soft snow.

    1. Approach the bump; sink down, and plant the pole.

    2. Rise up and forward and expect to be slightly airborne. As the tails are off

76

3

4

the snow they can easily be displaced or "hopped" away from the direction of the turn.

3. If the backside of the bump is not too slippery your skis will hold as they come back to earth and you drive your knees into the turn.

4. Completed turns are important in bumpy terrain so that your speed is kept down. Be sure to keep both hands ahead of you. Be ready! Bumps don't always fall into a convenient pattern.

very elegant pivoting of the skis, but at higher speeds the mogul turns into a jump and your up motion throws you into the air."[2]

If your goal is to ski faster and more smoothly (and I hope it is), you will have to dig deeper into your already large bag of tricks.

How should I try to unweight?

Take advantage of the fact that a bump is indeed a bump. When you were first learning anticipation, I suggested that you stand right on a bump to feel how easy it is to turn your skis where there is very little resistance. Stand on a bump again and see how you can swivel your feet back and forth. Just steer your skis one way and then the other.

In bumps you don't need to worry as much about unweighting. The act of skiing up and over a bump is almost exactly the same as sinking "down" and coming "up." In other words, if you let it, a bump will unweight *for* you. Try to think of every bump as a spot where you can make a turn with hardly any effort at all.

That is what is called "terrain unweighting," right?

Precisely. Skiing in bumps is a little like being a glider pilot. Every time you get an updraft—a lift from a bump—you should take advantage of it. Don't waste it. If you *miss* turning on two or three bumps in a row, you are being bounced around by them. So try to turn on every bump you can.

Ski slowly at first—very relaxed. Ski up to a bump, feel the lift, and swivel your feet. It's that simple. Ski down, up the side of another, and steer your feet in another direction, accepting whatever pattern the moguls happen to fall into. Sometimes it will help you to step up, or even make a

---

[2] Joubert, p. 119

couple of quick skating steps uphill, to give yourself a slightly better line on the next bump.

Why do some people say that this "foot swivel" is bad?

It isn't so bad in itself. You *should* be using your feet to pivot your skis a lot by now. "Foot swivel" is fine when the snow is good. My main objection would be that just "playing" in the moguls like this can make you awfully lazy. You are not being forced to use your legs, your edges, and your upper body very much.

"Foot swivel" is impossible unless you are standing fairly straight over the center of your skis, and unless your skis are almost perfectly flat on the snow. It is easy to fall into the habit of drifting listlessly down the back side of a mogul in this very high, nonchalant position. Swiveling your feet is okay as long as you keep working on "carving" rather than skidding through the *completion* of the turn. A combination of "foot swivel" and "down unweighting" is effective on the crest of a bump. By dropping to unweight, you can also be putting your skis on edge.

If your skis are *not* enough on edge when it gets icy and steep, you will find yourself slamming sideways into the valleys between the bumps, and will be unable to hold your line toward the next bump.

What's the smoothest way to ski in bumps?

That's easy; with anticipation. Anticipation is a beautiful technique for bumps because you unweight to the side instead of up.

But in order not to get jolted by it before the turn, you are going to have to absorb the bump with your legs and body (#1-#3 in Fig. 18). Plant your pole near the top of the bump while you twist your upper body

1

FIGURE 18: *Anticipation on a bump.* Anticipation has sometimes been described as a *pre*-rotation because the upper body turns before the skis do (see Chapter 4). In bumps, anticipation, *reploiment*—allowing the legs to absorb or "suck up" a bump—and terrain unweighting all work hand in hand to help a very good skier flow smoothly over moguls and keep his skis in contact with the snow.

    1. As the skier approaches this bump his upper body is still "square." That is, he has not yet started to anticipate. At this point he is getting ready to plant his pole near the top of the mogul.

    2. Now the upper body has twisted in the direction of the turn. See how the

torso is out of alignment with the skis? The upper body is stabilized by the pole plant. Notice too how the legs have bent to take up the shock of hitting the bump.

3. On the very crest of the mogul only a small portion of the skis is actually touching the snow. See how the tips and tails are free? This makes it very easy to release the edges . . .

4. . . . . and for lower-body alignment to take place.

5. Don't forget: anticipation only helps you *start* your turn. It will only bring you toward the fall line. The rest of the turn—as always—must be completed by actively steering with the legs. This edges the skis and makes them carve.

81

downhill (#2). As you release the edges, alignment will take place even more easily than before—because you *are* on a bump.

The most beautiful thing of all is that the skis stay on the snow all the way through the turn. If you are interested, the French call this leg shock absorption *reploiment*. That ought to be worth a few raised eyebrows back at the lodge.

What's the best way to slow down in the bumps?

Just skiing over a bump slows you down some. If you need to brake more, use a preturn. Unfortunately, in bumps you cannot make an edgeset in just any old place. I try to think of a field of bumps as a staircase. If you look closely, you will see that before the crest of each bump there is a flat place on the slope. The backside of each bump is like the riser of a step— even though the drop-off may not be entirely vertical.

Ski down the staircase, checking—with edgeset—on the flat part of each "step" (see #1 in Fig. 18), absorb and anticipate (#2), and complete the turn (#3-#5).

The bigger the bump, the steeper and icier its backside will be—because the downhill side of a bump is often shaded from the sun. Be sure, as before, to keep your skis on edge, to make a carved, completed turn. Don't forget to keep the outside hand coming around—"pushing open the door"—and down *low* to assist your angulation.

By the time you have completed one turn, you should already know exactly where you are going to preturn for the next.

What about jet turns in bumps?

Go ahead! I think it is easier to make good jet turns in bumps than it is where it is smooth. If you are going pretty fast, you can really feel the "compression" when you set your edges against the "flat step" (#2-#3 in Fig. 19). Be sure that you are not sitting back at this point, or your tips will fly up. You might end up on your fanny. Let your anticipated upper body continue ahead as your feet slow down (#3) to get the full benefit of rebound and jetting. Don't forget to "wait" for your feet to catch up (#4), and be sure that you are turning far enough out of the fall line to slow down. (You have heard me say that before and will hear it again.) Always, like the figure in the illustration, try to be looking where you are going.

Doesn't skiing with such severe edgeset look awfully jerky?

Yes. Abrupt edgesets *are* jerky. But you need them where it is steep. The trick is not to edge more than you have to. The very good skier uses only as much edgeset as he needs—in the same way that he uses only as much unweighting motion as he needs. You may have noticed that the very best skiers try to keep from getting their skis *across* the line of travel as much as they can. They try to avoid abrupt edgesets and sideslips, keeping their turns "pure" even in icy moguls. This is done by absorbing and anticipating more, while checking and jetting less.

It will help you to examine your own tracks when the snow permits. Compare yours to others. If your tracks make a broader pattern than most others (not *wider* in terms of your feet being farther apart), you are slipping sideways too much and "carving" too little. Your tracks through the arc of the turn should be narrow, proving that your skis are always pointing close to the line of travel.

Better still, if you can, follow a very good skier through some bumps. Try to keep up, and try to make your skis follow the line that his take. Everyone's line, like everyone's style, is unique, but it is a good exercise to imitate someone who skis better than you do.

FIGURE 19: *Jet turn on a bump with anticipation.* Neither photos nor illustrations ever seem to show how steep a slope really is. This sequence shows the demonstrator on the National at Stowe skiing at fairly high speed. All of the action in these six pictures took place in just a little more than a second.

1. As he nears the bump the skier's eyes are focused on that flat spot near the crest of the mogul where he can effectively check by setting his edges. See how the upper body has begun to anticipate the turn.

2. Here the edges are set.

3. Look at the difference in the relationship between the feet and the rest of the body in #2 and #3. In #2 the feet are right beneath the hips. In #3 they are slightly ahead. This is because the skis have jetted as a result of the hard edge-set. They almost seem to ricochet off the bump. The upper body shows *extreme* anticipation. Rather than be thrown backward and off balance by the jetting action, the skier will take advantage of it—as well as the anticipation—and quickly pivot the skis into the fall line.

4. Here body realignment is taking place. The lower body is seeking the position that the upper body established *before* the turn. The muscles in the legs have already "rebounded."

5–6. Now the knees really begin to drive forward to complete the turn. Notice how the eyes are already focused on the terrain ahead where the next turn will be.

It is important to remember that rebound and anticipation only help you to get *to* the fall line. *Completing* the turn always means that the legs must work for you!

6

84

But how can I keep my turns "pure" and still control my speed enough in bumps?

I wish that I had a simple answer. I have never suggested that this is easy. Learning to "feel your edges," trusting that skiing right at and *up* the face of a mogul will slow you down, and skiing hundreds and hundreds of miles through bumps are the most obvious solutions. Yet somehow my just saying, "Practice!" seems to be a cop-out.

I guess the ultimate answer is that in bumps you have to become so experienced that you are like a hockey player who never thinks about skating, or like a basketball player who doesn't have to think about dribbling. The ability to check delicately and subtly—even unconsciously—will come *only* with practice.

In time, you will find yourself thinking about the total turn, about your line, and about the bumps ahead of you. Once you "feel the snow" to the extent that you are forgetting about the actual mechanics of unweighting, checking, or planting your pole, you have got it made. All of this will take time.

When you have made a series of good turns, and later cannot recall whether you were trying to swivel your feet, anticipate, or jet, you will have at last moved out of the realm of technique and begun to establish a style all your own. When that happens, you won't need my help any longer.

Then will I be able to "ski with the big boys"?

With some of them. There will always be some that none of us can ever hope to keep up with. For now, what is more important is that you are ready to go and play on the slopes where the big boys play. The next chapters will tell you how.

6 Big Moguls

Moguls—*big* moguls, not little bumps—are a fact of life for the very good skier. Wishing them away, wishing they were smaller, or wishing they were shaped differently doesn't help much. In fact, except when they are "impossibly" shaped, moguls are psychological hazards more than physical ones. A skier's psychological approach to skiing in big bumps—believing, for instance, that a bump can be a help rather than a hindrance—is every bit as important as his directional approach to bumpy terrain.

All moguls are formed because skiers, like most humans, are conformists. Everyone seems to want to turn where the guy in front of him turned. On a day when there has been new snow it is amazing to see how people's tracks seem to follow others. Because everyone is turning in just about the same place, the snow gets scraped from there and is pushed somewhere else, forming a mound. The mound, in time—and in heavy traffic—hardens and becomes a mogul.

The most obvious approach to skiing in big moguls is to ski *around* them all the time. The idea is that if you can avoid the bumps themselves, you are skiing on smooth ground with a few psychological hazards that get in the way every so often. This "trough theory"—a "trough" is the flat place between waves, or bumps, or moguls—only works for a while. The trough can be more like a canyon than a flat place, and sooner or later a big fat mogul looms up in front of you. You are forced to ski up and over it, and to make a turn at the same time. This is usually when the trouble starts.

To make matters worse, because everybody is trying to ski in the trough, the trough is where the worst snow is. The trough becomes icy as soon as the new snow is pushed out. The pretty good skier comes through the bumps—gritting his teeth a lot, usually—making scraping noises with his edges as he tries to cope with the ice in the trough. The *very* good skier, on the other hand, comes through the same passage of bumps making very little noise. He sometimes turns on the *tops* of the bumps, where the snow is better. Then he skis down and across the trough without trying to edge his skis too much, skis up to the top of another mogul, turns on the good snow again, and keeps going. Obviously the very good skier is having more fun. Because his line is better, and because he is more confident, he gets through the difficult places with less effort.

Large, icy, poorly shaped moguls separate the pretty good skiers from the very good ones. If you are a pretty good skier who can ski well where it is steep, or even where there are small bumps on a steep slope, but find that you are slightly off balance or unable to establish any rhythm for yourself in a field of big bumps, join the club. All good skiers sometimes share your frustration. Maybe some of the suggestions in this chapter will help.

BIG MOGULS

What's the most important single thing to remember when I'm in big bumps?

To be as loose and relaxed as possible at all times. If your body is too tense or your mental approach to a given series of bumps is too rigidly planned ahead of time, you are licked before you start. Try to be ready—both in your stance and in your mental attitude—for anything. Be alert but be confident. Try to remember that you are already a good skier.

You keep telling me to relax, but that's not so easy for me if I'm frightened! What else do you suggest?

You are right. It is always easy to tell somebody else to relax. We will be talking about fear and how it can effect skiers in another chapter. For now, instead of thinking about how horrible the bumps are, think about trying to keep your skis on the snow as much as possible. The more of the total length of the skis you can keep in contact with the snow, the better off you will be.

How will that help?

Big moguls—as you have probably discovered—tend to throw you into the air and back onto the tails of your skis. If you are sitting back too far and have flown off the snow, you have *no* control and will probably crash. Your body will *have* to be relaxed if you are going to maintain contact with the snow. If you concentrate on just this much at first, you are on the right track.

89

What's the best way to keep my skis on the snow all the time?

Use the "gorilla stance" and let your *whole* body absorb the bumps—not just your legs. Try skiing over some bumps first without trying to make any turns (see Chapter 1). I have had success on the hill telling people that skiing in the very big bumps is a little like being raped. If you can make yourself relax and enjoy it, it is much more fun. The analogy is shocking, but people seem to get the point and remember it. Try to let your body be as passive as possible. As the bump approaches, allow it to come up under you, forcing your knees up. Let your body collapse as you pass over the top.

If you relax and enjoy it, that's hardly rape!

Exactly! And no one is suggesting that real rape should be fun. But you *do* let big bumps "rape" you in a sense, if you fight them. You get jolted and thrown off balance. Being passive loosens the joints so that the whole body acts like a shock absorber.

Isn't there a name for this technique?

Yes. Technical terms are not usually important, but there is one that should be mentioned. The French, although they may or may not have been the first to do it, were the first to attach a name to it. They called it *avalement,* which means "swallowing." In the big bumps, the very good skier "swallows" the moguls with his body and is always able to keep his skis on the snow.

90

BIG MOGULS

*There has been so much written and said
about the French Technique and about* avalement
in particular that I'm confused.

Lots of people seem to be confused about *avalement. Avalement* actually has nothing to do with turning. It is simply a way of absorbing irregularities in terrain, like ruts and moguls. You do it by retracting your legs and at the same time tightening your stomach muscles so that the upper body tips forward.[1]

Doesn't avalement *have something to do
with sitting back?*

No. *Avalement* has nothing to do with sitting back, although sometimes it may appear that way. *Avalement* is movement between two relatively extreme positions. The first is what we have already called an "extended" position (see #1, #7 and #13 in Fig. 20). This is the natural, slightly slouched "gorilla position" that I hope is your normal stance by now. The other extreme is what is called a "compressed" position (#5 and #11). Here the body has been collapsed by a mogul. It has folded at all the joints—ankles, knees, back and neck have all flexed or rounded.

Because of the way our bodies are constructed, when we are "compressed," the knees come up, and we appear to be sitting back. Actually it is sort of an optical illusion. If you look carefully at the very best skiers, you will see that even as they are "compressed" they are still pressing forward *from the knees down.* They are still applying pressure to the tips of the skis and staying under control that way.

[1] Abraham, p. 4.

91

FIGURE 20: *"Squatty-body turn" (S-turn with avalement)*. If a prospective student approaches a ski-school desk and says, "I want to learn *avalement*," the chances are pretty good that he wants to know how to make this kind of move in big bumps. He might call them "compression turns" or "retraction turns." He might even be confused enough to call this "down unweighting."

The teacher on the hill may have to straighten out his terminology. Then he will probably have to teach two things before he teaches the squatty-body: the concept of anticipation, and *avalement*—terrain absorption involving the whole body, which has nothing whatever to do with turning. Here is how an S-turn with *avalement* might be demonstrated:

1. This is the demonstrator's natural athletic stance—high, relaxed and confident.

2. As he approaches a mogul he does not tense, but starts to go limp. All of the joints in his body are loose—ready to flex.

3. The right hand gets ready for the pole plant.

4. As the pole is planted the upper body starts to anticipate. At the same time the legs bend to absorb the bump and the torso tips ahead to aid in the absorption and keep the center of gravity over the *middle of the skis*.

5. This is the point of most "compression" (absorption) on the top of this first small mogul. The illusion here is that the skier is sitting back. But look carefully at the legs. Notice how the knee is forward of the ankle bone. Here—as well as in #11—the skier is maintaining even pressure against the fronts of the boots and, in turn, against the shovel section of the skis.

6. Now the skis align with the upper body with the help of foot and leg steering. The body quickly extends so that the skis do not lose contact with the snow.

7. This is the point of maximum "extension." The demonstrator is standing as "tall" here as at any point in the sequence.

8. He flexes again to be ready for the very large mogul ahead.

9. Now the upper body begins to anticipate again . . .

10. . . . and the feet are pushed ahead ever so gently.

11. The whole body has collapsed very quickly because of the steepness and sharpness of the mogul. Is the skier sitting back here? In relation to a level horizon, he is, yes. But in relation to the face of the mogul he is not. (Look at the lower leg again.) Is a sailboat which is moving up the side of a great wave "sitting back" because its mast is not perfectly vertical?

(Continued on page 94)

92

12. As lower body alignment happens, the skier must extend vigorously to "fill in the hole" in the back side of the mogul with his feet. Because he has gained some speed on this steep slope . . .

13. . . . he almost banks to complete the turn . . .

14. . . . and skis out of the picture.

But don't I see pictures of racers sitting back?

Yes. Unfortunately you probably have. It makes a spectacular picture to show a racer recovering from a mistake—which they often do. More than one fine ski teacher has complained about a ski photographer's tendency to show this. One has remarked about posters and ski magazines: "Racers, for instance, are shown in recovery phases, life size. The laymen made a technique out of it! 'The French sit back and plant the pole behind the heels,' was only one bit of misinformation."[2]

You mean that racers and very good skiers never sit back on purpose?

That is not entirely true either. Racers often sit back in flat sections of courses to make their skis run faster. When they do, they are consciously carving turns with the tails of the skis. We will discuss this in another chapter too. Lots of very good recreational skiers also sit back at times. It really doesn't work very well where it is steep, icy, and bumpy. Here the very good skiers try to stay forward or over the middle of their skis. You should try to do the same.

[2] Abraham, p. 1.

94

BIG MOGULS

But don't the hotshots sit back even in the bumps on the very steepest slopes?

Yes, they do. They sit way back on their tails as they approach a bump, and allow the skis to accelerate. The tips seem to be exploded off the bump and into the air as the skier does a sort of "wheelie" or "windshield-wiper" turn. This sort of acrobatic exercise, although it is spectacular and especially attractive to younger skiers, is really little more than a series of linked recoveries down the side of the mountain. These "super jet turns"—they are actually not jet turns, as we have seen—are dangerous, tiring, and recommended only for the young and fearless. It is flamboyant style, and has nothing to do with good technique.

What is this we read and hear about pushing the feet ahead?

This, along with the development of the high-backed boots, is what has been the source of so much confusion among good skiers. The French, as they developed the concept of *avalement,* began pushing their feet ahead (very gently, *very* briefly, and very subtly) just as they were about to ski over a large mogul or a rut in a slalom course (#3 and #9 in Fig. 20). Ski photographers caught some of the French team members just at this split-second before the body was fully compressed. All of a sudden somebody decided that the French were now sitting back, and every hotshot kid in the world started trying to ski that way *all the time.*[3]

[3] Joubert, p. 126.

95

Why do some very good skiers push their feet ahead as they are about to use avalement *on a bump?*

For two very good reasons. If a skier edges and applies gentle pressure to the tails of the skis (without sitting *way* back and being thrown off balance as he skis up the side of a mogul), the tips of the skis will tend to turn back up the hill ever so slightly. This is an effective way of subtly and smoothly checking speed without an abrupt edgeset. This, and the fact that the skis are traveling uphill as they go up the steep side of a mogul, results in considerable braking.

More important, letting the feet come forward a little "increases absorption amplitude."[4] In other words, it *is possible to compress the body from this sitting position a bit more if the feet are a little bit ahead of you. As the bump causes the knees to retract and the stomach muscles pull the upper body forward, the feet catch up to the upper body at the crest of the bump (#5 and #11 in Fig. 20).*

Should I try that?

Not right away. At first if you want to slow yourself down on the near side of a bump, use a conventional edgeset or preturn. (Remember the staircase exercise in Chapter 5.) Later, when you seem to be making good turns with *avalement* in the bigger bumps, experiment with pushing your feet ahead—very carefully!—as you approach the steep face of a high mogul.

[4] Abraham, p. 37.

BIG MOGULS

All right. If I can ski over the big moguls and keep my skis on the snow, how do I go about turning?

Now you are ready for "squatty-body" turns. This term is often used to describe smooth "S" turns in big bumps. The squatty-body turn is a turn on or near the crest of a sharp mogul using the mogul itself for un-weighting, extreme absorption *(avalement)*, and anticipation.

How do I do one?

Practice anticipation turns on a smooth slope and on small moguls before you try to make squatty-body turns in the big ones. Then begin by skiing *very* slowly in the big bumps. As you ski toward the first large mo-gul, stand in your normal extended stance. As your tips begin to climb the face of the mogul, allow your body to begin its compression. All joints want to flex at the same time.

How is this different from what we've been doing?

It's not. But now, instead of facing your upper body ahead of you (to-ward the other side of the mogul), turn and face yourself *downhill* (that is the way you are going to be turning), and plant your downhill pole (#4-#5; #9-#10 in Fig. 20). This is just "anticipation." As you reach the crest of the mogul (your body will have been compressing all this time), you will feel your skis want to pivot in the direction you are turn-ing—to align themselves with the anticipated upper body (#5-#6 and #11-#12)—just the way they did in the smaller bumps.

This is the most critical point in the turn. Starting the turn is easy enough—anticipation and the bump itself have taken care of that. Now you must *complete* the turn. At the same time you have to keep your skis on the snow.

Weight your outside ski, and push your knees in the direction you want to go (#7–#8 and #12–#13), while you allow your body to *extend* again (#6–#7 and #12–#13). This extension is up *weighting*. It should feel as though you are aggressively pushing your feet into a hole on the backside of the mogul.

What can go wrong?

Probably nothing too serious if you understand anticipation and *avalement* and can make them work. Most of your initial mistakes will have to do with timing and coordinating all of the movements. Unless you put things together pretty well (which will take some time and practice), you may have trouble absorbing the bump properly and making a good turn at the same time. On the other hand, you may be surprised at how easy it is to turn the skis with this technique.

Why do I feel off balance and out of control at the end of the turn?

Probably because you *are* off balance and out of control, at least temporarily. Because your timing is not exactly right, you are still being "raped" a little by the mogul. Remember that the mogul may drop away very suddenly on the backside. Be sure that everything is well forward by the time you reach the crest. You can't afford to be off balance even for a split-second.

BIG MOGULS

When I get to the point on the top of the mogul where I am most compressed, I find that I am looking down at my feet. How can I correct this?

You are right to remember that looking at your feet can get you into trouble. But it is particularly difficult to keep looking ahead when you are trying so hard to compress. This is a common complaint from those who are learning the squatty-body S-turn. Lots of people try to absorb a bump by bending at the waist too little and by ducking the head too much. Bending the waist is more important than rounding the neck. If you duck your head too much, you not only won't be able to see, you will feel your chin jam into the upper part of your chest—uncomfortable and distracting. Keep your chin up.

Is the pole plant really as critical as it seems? When I don't do it right, I really get caught off balance!

It *is* important, but it is no more important here than it has been in the other turns we have discussed. It is still a timing device, a getting-the-shoulders-in-the-right-position device, and a *steadying* device. But remember: just as in the anticipation turn, it must not be used as a crutch. If you are falling or nearly falling when you miss the pole plant (or when the pole skids), you are relying too much on the pole and may be leaning on it. Don't forget that you are in motion and that you are leaving the base of the crutch behind you. Stand on your own two feet. You'll get into all sorts of trouble if you lean on the pole.

I seem to have lost all rhythm. Why do I never seem ready for the next turn?

The position of large moguls on a slope is rarely rhythmical. In time, you will learn ways to build rhythm into your skiing, with or without the help of the terrain. Chapter 8, "Line, Strategy, and Fear," should help.

You may still be having trouble because you are leaving your pole in the snow too long. Remember to keep yourself facing the way you are going (or are *about* to go), and keep both hands in sight at all times. If you leave the pole planted too long, your inside hand is going to be pulled back behind you, and your forward-looking position will be destroyed. By the time you recover, it may be too late.

Remember to keep your pole plant simple, quick, and unobtrusive. Anything fancy is not only unnecessary, but takes too long and will throw your rhythm off.

What next?

That is up to you. Mileage in the big bumps, mostly. More speed. More confidence. *Style.* Now you should be able to start really putting things together. But use this squatty-body turn sparingly. To make a run doing nothing but squatty-bodies looks ridiculous. It is also exhausting.

Ski in the trough when the snow looks good there. Check your speed on the "flat" parts of the "staircase." Use conventional parallel turns and jet turns where it seems right. Show all of your moves. But don't shy away from the big moguls when they get in your way. You know how to cope with them.

BIG MOGULS

How will I know when I am skiing well in the big bumps?

You will know; don't worry! But a "perfect" turn is an uncommon thing. You may make only a few of them in an entire season. When you do, you will remember it. The day that you make a very difficult run without being conscious of making a single mistake should be the day you decide to stop skiing forever.

A turn that looks perfect to somebody else (even to a very experienced skiing companion) will probably not feel perfect to you. Accept the fact that you are always going to make small errors. If in skiing bad moguls you experience some sort of relaxed and controlled fluidity, and feel that you and the bumps have somehow called a momentary truce with each other—even that your body and a single given mogul have briefly cooperated—and that through your own suppleness and skill, you and the skis have adapted reasonably smoothly to a devious and erratic set of bumps, you have learned—and *felt*—what it is to ski well in big moguls.

7 *Resting and Sitting Back*

Wouldn't it be great if we could ski our hardest all day long without getting tired? None of us can. Even Olympians have to rest. Some ski manuals and ski instructors—although the latter get tired themselves—seem to ignore the existence of fatigue. Sometimes, because of the cold, or because of the excitement of the day, it is difficult to recognize when we are getting tired ourselves. This is when skiing becomes most dangerous. Tired skiers begin to make little mistakes. And little mistakes can result in accidents.

Nobody wants to get hurt. When you find that you are crossing your tips a lot, that your timing is suddenly off, or that your legs just don't seem to have the strength to hold onto those slippery places anymore, stop and rest. Often. Don't try to be a hero. Don't try to keep up with friends who seem to be in better shape—a skier with weary legs who is trying to keep up with a faster group can get into trouble. Have lunch. Sit in the sun, or go have an ego-booster run on some easy slope.

RESTING AND SITTING BACK

Very good skiers, like cross-country skiers, learn how to pace themselves. They learn to rest without necessarily coming to a stop every few hundred feet. They learn how to relax one set of muscles while a different set is working. They learn how to ski differently on different snow conditions and on different sections of the mountain. They know that any skier who can "pound" down the steepest faces of the mountain all day long doing nothing but jet turns or squatty-body turns and still be strong when the lifts close is a rare one indeed.

Racers—skiing on longer and longer courses, at higher and higher speeds, and on better and better equipment—have proved that the old rules which used to govern ski technique no longer always apply. "Sitting" (back), "Standing" (up too straight), and "Leaning" (into the turn) used to be considered skiing's Three Cardinal Sins. Even the old adage about keeping all the weight on the downhill ski has been called into question. It is still not a good idea to stand up too straight. But there are times when sitting back or leaning into a turn can be helpful and restful.

Enjoy your day more—and get your money's worth out of your expensive all-day lift ticket—by learning some more of those modern body positions which the racers use. Learn how to "get away with technical murder" by doing things "wrong" and still staying under control. Resting can be more than fun—it can even look nice!

Where on the mountain should I be trying to rest?

On flat places. On smooth sections. Wherever the snow is especially good or wherever you feel particularly confident.

What are some good resting positions?

You can stretch your legs, arch your back, even wiggle your fanny a little to loosen up your middle, as long as the terrain is not too difficult

103

and you have no need to turn. Standing up straighter sometimes helps if you need to catch your breath.

Doing a kind of half-baked imitation of the downhill racer's "dynamic egg" position can be restful. Tuck your poles up under your arms so your forearms and hands can relax. Then bend over and rest your elbows on your knees. If you are going fairly fast, or if it is even a little bumpy, don't squat so much that you are sitting back. Some freakish accidents happen in the easiest places because good skiers have relaxed to much.

If it really is flat and smooth, it is fun to sit right down on the tails of your skis. Careful not to fall sideways! In fact, don't try this at all unless you are good and limber. If you have high boots—as well as good thigh and stomach muscles—you can pull yourself back up to a normal skiing stance.

Remember that all of these are resting *positions*. They are difficult to get out of quickly. Choose your spots and use them carefully.

Is there any way I can keep from getting so out of breath?

Are you remembering to breathe? That's no joke! If you are frightened, or concentrating very hard, you can unconsciously hold your breath. Lots of people do this. And it makes you get tired very fast.

Young racers have to be taught to keep breathing. Have you ever stood next to a giant slalom or downhill course and heard racers come by making exaggerated puffing noises? They are not so much out of breath as they are reminding themselves to breathe.

If you are certain that you *are* breathing—even through particularly difficult passages on the mountain—you must accept the fact that your lack of wind is an obvious bodily signal that you are not in as good shape as you might be. Skiing more often will surely help. Jogging in the fall probably wouldn't do a bit of harm either. Riding a bike would help too.

RESTING AND SITTING BACK

What's the best way to rest without posing?

There are several ways. Basically any substantial change in body position is going to be restful. Do something different. For example, if you are a person who skis very far forward over your tips (this is sometimes good), learn how you can use the *tails* of your skis more effectively by standing a little more flat-footed.

If you are someone who skis with his hands quite high, learn to drop them to relax the muscles in your arms. (Low hands are good too. They help to make you more stable by lowering your center of gravity.)

If you ski with lots of angulation (which is okay), learn to rest by "banking" sometimes.

What is "banking"?

Banking, in technical parlance, is called "inclination to the turn" (see Fig. 21). You simply allow your upper body to incline—or lean—the way you are going to turn. It is not anticipation because you do not twist your upper body first. The shoulders stay square to the skis.

Banking can be done with or without edgeset and with or without a definite unweighting motion. Good banked turns should be wide, flowing arcs. Anyone who is doing it is probably not making any effort to slow himself down.

What happens to your weight during banked turns?

To begin with, you might feel that you are standing on both skis instead of just the outside one. Later as you get better at banking, speed and centrifugal force may make you feel that you are skiing on the edge of your outside ski without your consciously putting weight there. If your

FIGURE 21: *Pure banking.* Making turns by banking is a fun way to ski. People who try it for the first time often say that they feel like an airplane. Because banking violates some of the basic fundamentals of good ski technique it should be regarded as a resting maneuver, and should be used only where there is flat terrain and good snow.

1. To start a banked turn step onto your uphill ski and allow your body to incline—or lean—the way you want to go. Your skis will start to point themselves at the fall line.

2. Leaning to the inside this way gets the center of your body mass way *inside* the turn's arc, instead of over the outside ski where it would normally be. (Here the demonstrator in the illustration has very little control over the radius of the turn as a result. All he can do is allow the skis to do their own thing according to the way they were designed.)

3. When you pass the fall line you step to the new uphill ski and . . .

4. . . . lean down the hill again. At this rather unsteady point you may want to use your pole briefly as a third point of contact with the snow to help you balance.

5. In its purest form banking requires no unweighting. Just bending the knees and leaning to the inside puts the skis on edge . . .

6. . . . so that they will practically turn on their own. You just enjoy the ride.

Don't be surprised if you are unable to follow the tracks of someone ahead of you who is also making banked turns. If his skis are slightly longer (or shorter), cut differently, or flex differently than yours do, the pattern of his turns may be quite different.

106

1

2

3

4

5

6

107

skis are doing all the right things as you bank, you will feel pressure first against one big toe—on the outside foot—and then the other as you change direction and go the other way. (Remember the exercise for up weighting in chapter four, where you "pushed" against your big toe to turn?)

As you start a banked turn (#1 in Fig. 21) you step onto the uphill ski and incline your body downhill (#1–#2). When you pass the fall line (#3), you step on the new uphill ski and lean downhill again (#4). What you are doing will look like a maneuver on water skis. It is most fun if you do not try to link turns together too closely.

What about unweighting?

In its purest form, banking does not require any unweighting. Just bending the knees and leaning to the side puts your skis on edge enough so that they will practically turn on their own. (Notice that the turns in Fig. 21 are done without unweighting.)

Sometimes, if the snow does not feel just right, you may want to unweight a little too (look at the "down-up" in Fig. 22). The turn can be finished with banking instead of a "down and in" knee crank. Remember to keep your shoulders square by letting them rotate as fast as the skis turn. Because the arc of a banked turn is usually a wide one, it is easy to get caught in a counter-rotated pose—not an incorrect position, but an obsolete one.

Can't leaning to the inside like this get me into trouble?

Yes, it can. That is the best argument for using pure banking only in near-perfect conditions. Pure banking contradicts traditional skiing principles. And you *can* get caught off balance and be unable to recover.

Leaning to the inside (#2 in Fig. 21) gets the center of your body mass *inside* the turn's arc instead of *over* the outside ski where it would normally be. What this means is that if you were in this position (#2) and your skis were flat on the snow—stiff modern boots prevent this, fortunately—the automatic result would be a sideslip which you could not control. By keeping your ankles stiff and keeping your skis on edge, your boots allow you to hang on by the very "skin" of your outside edge. Sometimes there is a very fine line between hanging on and falling on your inside hip.

Be sure that you have lots of confidence in your skis' ability to hold on the snow before you commit yourself to an extreme inward lean.

Why can't I control the arc of my turns so well when I am banking?

Once you step to that uphill ski and lean downhill, your turn has begun. From this point on, until you pass throught the fall line and get ready to shift your weight again, you are at the mercy of forces over which you have little control.

Unless you have extraordinary feel for the particular pair of skis you are using, the arc of the turn is being determined by your speed, by the amount of frictional resistance to sideslipping in the snow, and by the flex pattern and "side cut"—shape—of your skis. All of this sounds suspiciously like ski-instructor jargon, I know.

Generally, a ski that is flexibly "soft," wide at the "shovel" (that's the part near the tip), and very narrow at the "waist" (somewhere under your foot) will bank a turn more easily than a stiff ski which has a less radical variation in width. In fact, a ski that is engineered this way will make *all* kinds of turns more easily, although it will have some disadvantages too.

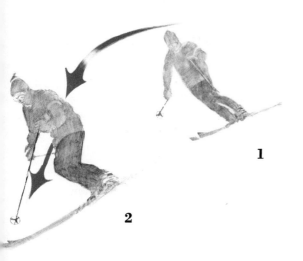

1

2

Figure 22: *Banking (with unweighting) and stepping.* As you begin to devise your own skiing style you will begin to use various techniques in combination. One of the marks of a truly expert skier is that it is difficult to distinguish exactly what technique he is using at any given time. This sequence—which is a continuation of the "pure" banking in Fig. 21— was drawn from actual photographs.

1. The demonstrator has just completed a "pure" banked turn. He is just beginning to step to the uphill ski.

2. But because the snow does not feel just right he senses that he will need to unweight a little for the next turn. He sinks down . . .

3. . . . and rises up. Now he begins to bank again.

4. The turn is continued—not with an abrupt down-and-in motion with the legs, but with an inward lean.

5. At this point either the skis start to slip or the skier is concerned that the turn is not going to be sharp enough (he was actually about to ski into the photographer). He directs the tip of the inside ski *farther* to the inside, puts it on edge by "hooking" his left knee, and steps to it.

6. This little step steers him farther uphill and allows him time to get his weight back over his skis. This is a good way to not only regain your balance but to make quick adjustments in your line as you ski through a field of moguls.

Racers often use a move like the one seen in #5. A vigorous push off the outside ski as the weight is shifted to the inside will help the racer to accelerate as well as improve his line.

But how can I make banked turns sharper?

You can sharpen your turns a little by driving your knees forward and in just the way you would in a normal parallel turn. This will feel like you are pushing a little harder with that outside big toe. A very good skier, manipulating that edge, might feel as though he were caressing the snow with the outside ski, with more or less pressure as he needs it.

But because you are *not* standing right over your skis (to be a little repetitious), you cannot regulate the turning radius all that much. Just relax and enjoy the swooping turns, letting your skis do their own thing.

Is there any way I can get out of trouble if I am caught off balance to the inside?

Don't be embarrassed to step out of a turn that is going badly for you, especially if you are tired. If you feel the skis starting to slip out from under you, step onto your edged uphill ski a little early (#5 in Fig. 22), and steer it uphill to allow yourself time to get your weight back over your skis (#6). This is a technique you might already use to adjust your line slightly in bumps.

Making a series of stepped turns—actually lifting the uphill ski off the snow to direct it before you weight it—is a good way to rest. Once you weight it, you can continue to turn on it while you relax those hard-working muscles in your outside leg.

A very good skier stepping gently uphill will "hook" his uphill knee (see #5 in Fig. 22 again) so that he looks bowlegged for an instant. Other very good skiers who are watching will appreciate what he is doing, and will not see this hooking as a mistake.

112

RESTING AND SITTING BACK

I think I understand banking. How do I learn to use the tails of my skis more effectively?

Modern skis are being designed with the "waist"—the narrowest part of the ski—farther and farther back toward the tail. This makes it possible to turn with the weight slightly back as well as forward. Mr Joubert recommends taking advantage of the ski's advanced design by learning to "carve with the tails." All good skis have a critical "pivot point" or "swing point," whether it is farther ahead or farther back. You would do well to experiment a bit, and learn to feel exactly where yours is in relation to your stance.

To find it, you may need to be standing, paradoxically, in an almost seated position. I feel as though I am standing flat-footed with my knees sticking out in front of me. You'll see what I mean if you try it. Try to "improve your sensitivity to what is happening under your skis, and use the pivot point to your advantage."[1] Settle back on the entire length of your foot so that you are able to pivot around the *binding* instead of around the tip.[2]

By rocking forward onto the balls of your feet or backward toward your heels, you can find a point where you can ski and swivel your feet without the help of unweighting or a bump.

How do I use this pivot point to my advantage?

Once you have discovered what it is like to be standing directly over the pivot point, you can become like a surfer who moves forward and back on his board depending on where he is situated on a wave.

Sometimes, to rest on the flat, you might sit back a little using the

[1] Joubert, p. 80.
[2] Abraham, p. 34.

113

FIGURE 23: *Sitting back.* Sitting back slightly to make better use of the ski's tail section is particularly effective on flat terrain or when the snow is less than ideal—"cruddy." ("Crud" might be powder with the consistency of wet concrete, heavy slush, wind slab, breakable crust, or a multitude of other nearly unskiable conditions.)

Carving with the tails allows you to keep the tips off the snow part of the time (see #2 and #4) and reduces the chances of getting an edge hung up in the bad snow.

In this sequence we see the demonstrator making two distinctly different turns, even though he is sitting back in both cases.

1. He sees tricky snow ahead and begins to rock gently backward in his boots.

2. He has applied enough pressure against the boot's high backs to make the tips of the skis rise off the snow (see the shadow). Notice how he has allowed his hips to move into a "low" position—somewhere behind his feet (in contrast to figure #5 where the hips are "high"—directly *above* the feet). The experienced skier will never commit himself to this low hip position so completely that he cannot re-

114

3   4   5

cover from it and pull himself forward again. Now he will "bank" his knees to the left and allow the tail configuration of the ski to help him initiate the turn.

3. As he finishes the turn (notice how the spray of snow indicates the carving of the tails), he pulls himself forward to a more neutral position nearer the middle of the skis.

4. In the second turn the skier uses a kind of pseudo-*avalement* to get his skis unstuck from the crud. It is almost as if he is absorbing an imaginary bump by retracting his legs and contracting his stomach muscles. To get added turning power he has even projected his hips slightly to the outside of the turn.

5. As soon as the turn develops he pulls himself forward so that he can use the ski's tip and shovel section again.

The most important thing to remember about sitting back: using the rear third of the ski can be helpful in *some* situations. But these situations may only total about 5 percent of your skiing time. The other 95 percent of the time try to remember that you have as much as six feet of ski attached to each boot. Why use only the last two feet of the ski when you can use it all?

rear two-thirds of the ski—the tail is much wider than the waist too, you'll notice—like the rudder on a boat.[3] Where it is steeper you will want to carve with your tips. When it is icy and you need more bite with your edges, you will want to use the entire length of your ski.

How do I turn in this sitting position?

To turn you can just "bank" your knees from side to side (see Fig. 23) and push against those big toes. Now, instead of feeling pressure against the fronts of your boots, you will feel pressure from the boots against the sides of your ankles. If you feel lots of pressure against the *backs* of your ankles, you are technically out of control. Always try to be in a position to move forward over your tips if you need to.

Why do I find it awfully hard to unweight when I am sitting back?

It *is* hard to come "up and forward" from this flat-footed position. It is not especially difficult to *down*-unweight. I find it helpful sometimes to pretend that there are imaginary bumps ahead of me that I must absorb. (See the *second* turn in Fig. 23.)

From the seated position (#3 in Fig. 23), down-unweight by using a kind of pseudo-*avalement*—retracting your legs and tipping forward with the help of your stomach muscles (#4). You might anticipate at the same time, while you plant your pole for balance. Then quickly steer your knees and feet in the direction of the turn. If you really need a sharp completion at this point, it will help to pull yourself forward over the tips (#5).

[3] Joubert, pp. 83, 84.

116

RESTING AND SITTING BACK

Is there any way to "check" speed when you are sitting back?

If you are in a situation where you are worried about building up a *lot* of speed, you'd better get forward!

You *can* check while you are sitting "in the chair"—sitting back slightly behind the pivot point. When you get ready to turn, turn your belly button downhill along with your upper body (anticipate) and then "sit" still deeper in the chair by lowering your fanny still more. As Abraham says, "lowering the hips and turning the seat uphill" results in an edgeset with the tails of the skis.[4] (See Chapter 3 again.)

"Jackknife" your body after the preturn—using *avalement*—and let your skis jet as the edges are released. Be ready for acceleration as you hit the fall line! Use the backs of your boots to pull yourself forward if you have to, so that you will be in a good position to initiate the next turn, Wedel this way if it is not too steep.

Incidentally, this is what the high-backed competition boots are designed for. They are to help you recover—to get forward again. *Not* to turn against!

That's really fun! Why do ski schools and even some coaches seem to resist teaching this?

They *don't* resist teaching this to everybody. But because so many people, given the new equipment and all the publicity about the "new technique," will try to learn some of these things before they are ready for them, good ski teachers and coaches emphasize basics first. Too many skiers, when they have felt how much fun it is to carve with the tails by

[4] Abraham, p. 33.

sitting back and banking with the knees, for instance, do not use these moves judiciously.

These are resting maneuvers, for the most part. They *are* lots of fun, but the very good skiers have learned to use them cautiously and in moderation. They will not work at all unless you have a good grasp of skiing fundamentals. They should not be used on very challenging terrain.

Do women sit back too much?

Lots of people have asked me this—most of them men. One very well known skiing authority once commented that women who have become world-class racers almost invariably are quite heavily muscled in the thighs and very well developed in the fanny. This does seem to be the case, although there have been lots of notable exceptions. Suzie Chaffee, the very pretty former American olympic downhiller who has more recently made a name for herself as a freestyle skier, comes to mind right away.

Some men have noticed this not totally unattractive characteristic in many very good female skiers, and have remarked to me that women must sit back more easily because they have "more weight back there." Obviously they are spending too much time studying the girls' physiques and too little time watching them ski. As I suggested earlier, very good skiers ski very much alike, regardless of their sex. At a distance it is sometimes difficult to distinguish the men from the women on the World Cup racing circuit. They are all more or less balanced over the middle of the skis most of the time.

How do I know exactly when to sit back and when to be forward?

Recently I was eavesdropping on the world champion of professional ski racing as he was working with a group of local junior racers on the slalom hill at Stowe. The hill is pretty flat near the top, comes over a knoll, and then drops away sharply to a long steep pitch. One of the kids asked this same question.

The pro answered, "Sit back all you like on the flats to rest and gain speed. But when you come over the knoll, check! Get forward, get forward some more, and then get forward more, and you *still* may not be far enough forward."

All of the super experts seem in agreement on one thing: you cannot sit back too much on a steep slope or you will continually be losing your balance in the fall line.

As always, I will give you no exact formula. It is up to you to decide when and where you have to pull yourself forward. Just as it is the right of every student to flunk in college, it is the right of every skier to experiment with his own limitations of balance and fatigue, to lose control, and to fall wherever he chooses. Let trial and error be your guide. But don't get hurt!

8

Line, Strategy, and Fear

It's only human to be afraid. Any skier who skis a lot on formidable terrain and claims that he is never afraid is either a liar or a fool. Fear is an important factor in everyone's skiing. Because there is a certain amount of danger attached to our sport, the emotions which surround it often translate themselves into physical errors. A frightened skier is likely to express his fear in at least one of several ways:

1. *His hands fly up, or back out of the field of vision.* This makes it difficult to keep his upper body in a good slouched position and results in posing.

2. *He tries to grip the snow with his toes.* Lots of people try to curl their toes back, like claws. This accomplishes nothing. It just causes the foot and leg muscles to stiffen and cramp.

3. *His downhill leg straightens.* This is the most common and most obvious manifestation of fear. If the leg is stiff, there is no way the ski can

120

be put on edge properly. A scared skier says to himself, however unconsciously, "God, if I'm going to fall, I want to at least fall to the closest side, not down *there!*" So he leans uphill. Trying to balance on the uphill ski on an icy precipice is next to impossible.

4. *He is too timid.* The natural reaction to something painful or scary is to shy or lean away from it. One of the ironies of skiing is that the more frightened you are, the more you must press *forward* against your boots—not like driving a car where you ease *back* on the accelerator when you are going too fast. The timid skier sits back, builds up even more speed, and is soon totally out of control.

5. *He is too aggressive.* An overly aggressive skier fights the snow instead of working with it. He overturns—*too* far out of the fall line. He uses exaggerated motions and useless gesticulations.

6. *He stems or abstems.* He may use either too little motion or too much of the wrong kind— like rotation.

7. *He tries to get forward only with his eyes.* Getting forward with your eyes because you know that you must be forward only results in too much bend at the waist. If you stick your fanny out this much, you are really sitting back.

Any athlete who does things which involve the risk of physical harm must learn to accept and cope with his own fear. He learns to concentrate in spite of it. The trick in skiing is to discover not whether you are afraid or not, but what it is you do wrong when you *are* frightened.

You know how to correct each of these errors. Now you must learn to say to yourself (as I must), "All right, this place frightens me. I know I am going to stiffen my downhill leg," and then do something about it. Nothing will improve your skiing more than learning to understand your own skiing personality to the point where you can anticipate your own mistakes.

All right. Here's a question I have been embarrassed to ask before: Why am I more frightened early in the morning?

I am surprised that more people don't figure this out for themselves. Nothing seems to work right on the first run of the day. You are stiff from the day before, you have been sitting on a windy lift, and your muscles are cold. It's no wonder you are afraid! No athlete, no dancer in the world could be expected to perform well without any sort of warm-up. Trying to make a fast first run down something like the National at eight-thirty in the morning is like coming out of the grandstand at Forest Hills to face Rod Laver.

Expect your first run to be lousy. Know that you are going to make mistakes. Ski slowly down some trail that is only moderately difficult. Just work on warming up. When you get to the bottom you can always say to yourself, "The first run never counts." Next run you won't be so uptight.

Which are more afraid, men or women?

Men often ski more aggressively than women. But this is sometimes *because* they are afraid, and lots of times they over do it, skiing poorly as a result. Women are generally more prudent. They seem to vocalize their fears about the mountain more easily and for this reason very often do better than their male companions on very difficult terrain. But this may be the only truly fair generalization I can make. I have had serious problems in scary places with both men and women. Sometimes I have had to be very gentle, and sometimes I have had to be very harsh—with members of either sex. I am not even convinced that overt fear is a factor of age necessarily.

To cop out just a little, let me say that fear depends almost entirely on the individual. Men in some occupations, for example, seem to worry more about their well-being than others. I had a client once who was a surgeon. He would throw his hands into the air and out of his own way whenever he thought he was about to fall. His biggest fear was that he might injure a finger. Understandable.

One day he sat down hard on a cylindrical package of Rol-Aids which he was carrying in his back pocket, and came away with a lovely black-and-purple bruise. (He claimed that "Rol-Aids" was imprinted in reverse on his backside, but I found that hard to believe.) He confessed to me a week or so later that he had limped uncomfortably around the operating table for several days, and that from then on he was going to worry less about his hands and more about his bottom. For some reason his skiing improved too!

I had thought for years that young mothers feel their responsibilities very keenly and ski overcautiously because of them. I rather simplistically attributed it to motherly hormones or something equally dumb. I was apparently wrong. Last year a most attractive lady in a bulky down-filled parka skied with me for an entire week. We skied very fast, over some of the most difficult terrain I could find, and she stayed practically glued to my tails the whole time. On the lift she frequently spoke of her young children. When we were saying goodbye on the last day, she said, "I'll send you a birth announcement. I'm seven months pregnant, you know."

I must have turned a little pale thinking of all the hard mileage I had just put her through. We had both fallen—she pretty hard a couple of times. She read my distress and added quickly, "I didn't tell you because I was afraid you'd slow down!"

Will I do better skiing with friends or by myself?

Skiing should be fun. It should never be a game of "chicken." If you have friends who are fun to ski with, ski with them. As soon as skiing with a group becomes a frightening game of "brinkmanship" or "one-upmanship"—as these subconsciously competitive situations often do—bow out gracefully.

I think that it is good to ski by yourself early in the day. When you begin to feel good, ski with others—on *your* terms if you can. Go where you like to go, at a speed that is comfortable for you. If you are the fastest skier in the group, slow down or find another group to ski with. "Togetherness" is no fun for any member of a group who is frightened or struggling to keep up.

Should I stop when I make a mistake?

Good question. It depends on how serious the mistake, and how much trouble you have gotten yourself into. It is easy enough to recover from most little mistakes if you know what you are doing.

If you goof in some dangerous spot, stop. Get yourself organized and start again. Stop and cool off if you get very angry or frustrated—it's a lot safer to be mad at yourself when you are standing still.

If you seem to be making the same mistake over and over again, and can't figure out why, ask someone for help. Fear can help you develop serious bad habits in a period of half an hour.

How can I improve my line on real expert slopes?

Concentration is vitally important to expert skiing. If a slope is very difficult, your line will require constant adjustment and revision, even while you are in motion. You might be able to decide beforehand whether you want to take an "aggressive" line—one that is faster and closer to the fall line—or a "conservative" line—a slower one with more completed turns.

But it is a mistake to stand at the top of a given pitch and say, "I am going to turn there, there, and there, on that mogul, and then beneath that tree." As I have said before, this kind of rigid planning rarely works. You know what they say about "best-laid plans."

I am absolutely convinced that the very first turn in a series is the most critical one. Concentrate just on it, and don't let yourself get "psyched" by the rest of the hill. If you make a good first turn, frequently everything will fall into place after that. If you blow the first turn, it is worth stopping and starting all over again.

Is there any way I can be sure my first turn will be a good one?

Make your first turn very deliberately, at slow speed. Decide to make it very *close* to where you are standing. In other words, don't make a long traverse first—that's bad strategy because it will give you too much time to think and get frightened. Once you have chosen where you will make it, think only about it.

It is a very good idea to make your very first turn a stem christie. Try it. You need very little speed, and it makes a very stable turn to start things off right. Other good skiers who are watching will notice and appreciate what you are doing.

What is the best way to approach a passage on the mountain which really frightens me?

Approach it twice. First make a slow reconnaissance run to learn the hazards and to get the "feel" of the most difficult places.

On the second run, once you are reasonably familiar with the scary place, try not to stop at the top of it for a long time, looking down. It is too easy to convince yourself that you can never make it down *that!* It is good psychological strategy to ski aggressively *at* and right *over* the top of a very difficult place. (Remember: great *speed* is not necessarily a sign of aggressiveness.[1] Lots of precise, determined turns *are*.)

Once you stop to rest, you will already be partway down the hardest part. You have not had to establish rhythm right from scratch, because you have carried rhythm from a relatively easy passage into a more difficult one. From there down it will not be so bad. But don't hesitate too long thinking about the rest of the run before you start again.

What do I do if I catch an edge in a difficult place?

If you catch the outside edge of your downhill ski a lot in good snow, you are probably not edging enough. Bend your downhill knee more. On the other hand, in "crud" (any kind of bad snow), where the snow itself is apt to be "catchy," keep your skis as flat as possible. In either case, if you do not get thrown too badly, you can regain your balance by stepping briefly onto your uphill ski.

If you catch an edge badly enough to make you seriously lose your balance to the downhill side, you can sometimes "go with it," if you are quick enough. Some catlike skiers will catch an edge, step to the uphill ski, and take advantage of the fact that they are falling downhill by making a quick banked turn—sometimes steadying themselves by putting a hand right down on the snow. This sort of great recovery only works some of the time. Don't be ashamed if you catch an edge and fall. We all do it.

How should I fall?

For a good skier, a fall is usually sudden and totally unexpected. The best approach is to know how *not* to fall.

[1] Abraham, p. 40.

126

Good skiers too often injure themselves by digging a knee or thumb into the snow and getting it wrenched. Any skier should know that it is very dangerous to fall by putting the knee down first. If you are going to steady yourself with your hand on the snow, keep your fist closed around your pole to protect that vulnerable thumb.

The safest way to fall is onto your fanny or hip. If you go into a real "eggbeater," try to relax and hope that your bindings will release. If you fall face-first and start to slide, roll your skis over you and get them down-hill from you to help brake—even if the bindings have released.

Lots of very good skiers—many of them old racers—don't wear safety straps for fear of getting clonked on the head by a windmilling ski during a fall. They would rather have that ski get away from them. I felt the same way, until a runaway ski of mine nearly wiped out a little girl. They are a pain in the neck, but wear safety straps. It's good social strategy.

Why do my tips sometimes cross even when I am not sitting back?

Sometimes your tips *will* suddenly and mysteriously cross on expert slopes. A very sharp "V" between two moguls can jam your tips together and make them cross. If it is very steep and you are skiing with your feet quite close together, you can edge your downhill ski suddenly and have it "hook" up underneath the tip of the uphill ski—an awkward situation at best! Sometimes you can simply "step" out of this predicament.

It is always bad strategy to lose contact with the snow—by jumping—for no practical reason. Having crossed your tips is one of those few times when jumping is a good idea. A very good skier can get into the air, un-cross his tips, land, and keep on going without anyone taking notice.

Are there any other "practical" reasons for jumping?

A "prejump" is a good maneuver to develop if you are going to be skiing in "impossible" moguls. When you are confronted with a large undercut mogul with an insurmountable wall-like face, you may want to jump before you get to it, so you can land more or less gracefully on the top of the bump, turn, and ski down the backside. At high speed, a prejump which skims you over the top of a steep mogul can help you avoid being catapulted into the air.

A skier jumping from the top of one mogul, over a particularly fearsome trough, to the top or backside of another is a pretty sight. Again, he is doing it not to look spectacular, but to stay out of trouble.

What is the best line in these kinds of moguls?

There is no single "best route" out of such a labyrinth. Stick to whatever sort of line best suits your style.

But where the bumps become especially intimidating, it is better not to challenge them head-on. Instead of going right over a mogul's peak, for instance, make a turn on one of its lower shoulders. If your skis are reasonably soft in the tips, you will be amazed at how much they can bend and flex to accommodate the terrain as you ski over moguls. Remember not to stiffen your body as you approach a bump's wall in front of you. Be ready to collapse, and trust that your tips will ride up over it. They almost always will.

Use the trough. Sometimes you can bank turns off the sides of bumps,[2] as though you were on a bobsled run. And don't forget how valuable quick stepped turns can be.

[2] Joubert, p. 138.

LINE, STRATEGY, AND FEAR

What do I do if the back of a mogul drops off so suddenly that I cannot keep my skis on the snow?

To extend or not to extend, that is the question here. You need to make a quick decision. Normally you would up-weight at this point. Try not to literally overextend yourself. If you do, and drop stiffly into the trough, you will have a spine-crunching landing.

If it appears that there is no way you can stay in contact with the snow by extending, absorb the mogul as best you can, extend only slightly, and then relax as you drop, so that you land in a partially collapsed "gorilla stance" and can absorb the shock. Try not to balk just before one of these drop-offs. Stay forward and don't let your tips fly up.

What line do you suggest in badly shaped moguls where there is no rhythm?

Moguls are at their worst where there have been lots of weaker skiers skiing on a slope that is too hard for them. These skiers, because they are apt to traverse, reshape otherwise good moguls and destroy whatever "aggressive" rhythm might be there. This often happens wherever good skiers and not-so-good skiers must take a common route to their respective slopes.

Slow down and accept the more conservative line the weaker skiers have made. Down weighting and down unweighting will make you quicker on your feet. Down-unweight on the tops of rises, and push your feet down into the troughs and ruts. Get your hands out front and think about what you are doing, even if it is not especially steep. Don't be upset if you make one or two bad turns. If you are nice and loose and can keep your skis on the snow—even in the bottom of a sharp trough between moguls—you can make an unrhythmical place look rhythmical.

129

What about trying to keep my feet together?

Never put your feet together at the top of a descent and vow to make everything work from that position. It never works. As parallel skiers become more and more proficient, their skis naturally come closer and closer together. This is predictable and good. But *locking* the feet together prohibits "independent leg action."

If you always try to make both skis operate in unison, you can get into situations where you cannot react instantaneously. Double your balancing possibilities, and double your edging power, by at least allowing yourself the option of going into a "wide-track" stance when you need to. If you want to see what it feels like, try a few toilet-bowl turns, gripping your ankles as shown in Fig. 24.

Does slope strategy change with changes in snow conditions?

You bet it does! Never assume that all snow conditions require the same line. A slope with changed snow conditions today is an entirely different slope from what it was yesterday. This is another one of those things that makes skiing interesting. (Two extremes in snow conditions will be discussed in Chapter 9, "Powder," and Chapter 10, "Ice.")

In wet snows like slush or "mashed potatoes" (heavy, wet powder) or "windslab" (wind-packed snow), your line must become more aggressive. You will need to exaggerate your unweighting movements, and understate all edging motions. In this kind of "crud" you are leaving yourself wide open for catching an edge whenever you get your skis across the line of travel.

On faster "corn snow"—granular slush that is in the process of freezing—or fallen sleet, your line must be more conservative. You will need to complete your turns well out of the fall line.

130

FIGURE 24: *Toilet-bowl turns.* My good friend Peter Duke of Killington, Vermont, used to get bugged by skiers who would ski with their feet locked so tightly together that they had no feeling for good independent leg action. "Too many people are hung up on the concept of parallelity which insists that both skis operate simultaneously," he would grumble. "Too often they end up using their upper bodies to turn the skis rather than their legs and feet."

Peter started having people make turns while holding onto their ankles at the boot tops. This automatically seemed to accomplish two things:

First, it made people turn *only* with their legs and feet. (In this position the upper body is "blocked"—unable to move—which means that it can't assist the lower body in any way.)

Second, it forced them to ski with their legs and feet farther apart. (Ski technicians, by the way, are almost universally convinced that skis are *much* easier to turn when they are slightly separated than they are when they are right together.)

Many advanced skiers are annoyed when they are asked to make these toilet-bowl turns. "I can't turn that way!" seems to be a typical response. Almost invariably they *can* turn that way and do so immediately. Their skis come apart and—Heaven forbid as far as they are concerned—may become slightly out of parallel. But most can appreciate the idea that—perhaps for the first time in their skiing careers—they are really using their lower limbs the way they should to make the skis turn properly.

131

Springtime—that proverbially best time to ski—can be particularly treacherous. The conditions are rarely consistent. On one side of a slope you might find wet, cementlike slush, and slick "frozen granular" on the other side where it is shady. You must keep looking and thinking ahead.

"Breakable crust" presents a very tricky and hazardous problem. My advice is to stay out of it if you can, unless you are very confident and very powerful. If you do get caught in it, you may find that the only way you can release your edges is by jumping—getting the whole length of your skis off (out of) the surface of the snow. I have seen many a wise and experienced professional traverse and kickturn, traverse and kickturn through a field of breakable crust. That's the safest line.

What about different strategy in different types of weather?

Go out and ski in all kinds of snow in all kinds of weather. Don't bitch about it; ski it. It's the only way to learn. You will often find great skiing on those ostensibly miserable days.

Equip yourself for super-cold, windy days. The *snow* is usually fine. I have had some of my most memorable good days when it was raining and everyone was inside complaining. Snow conditions on rainy days are usually uniform, it is almost never icy, and oddly enough, rarely slushy. A rainsuit and "sou'wester" are a good investment for any serious skier.

It's always good fun to ski in a snowstorm, but you should never "bash"—ski too aggressively—because of the poor visibility. The new snow is nice, but it covers many dangers—like rocks and ice. Don't let it give you a false sense of security. Skiers who can ski by the "Braille system"— by feeling what is happening under their skis—do best in blizzards, in fog, and in "flat lighting" where it is hard to see bumps.

Be careful in moguls on foggy days when the temperature is well above 32 degrees. Snow tends to "rot" in the fog—melting from within. A mogul that is hard in the morning can turn into a pile of mush by lunch-time. You can unexpectedly drive your tips into it, and that sudden stop can hurt!

Why is it that I can have a run that feels so good followed by an absolutely terrible one on the same trail?

This is one of those frustrating mysteries that all very good skiers en-counter. The boundary between a "good" run and a "bad" one is a very frail one. Your "absolutely terrible" run was probably not as bad as you think. You always feel your mistakes much more intensely than someone watching you can see them.

But I know exactly what you mean. The contrast between back-to-back runs can be staggering. It is just a matter of being a fraction of an inch off; of having your skis on edge a tenth of a degree too much. It must have something to do with the chilling ride back up the mountain, with the fact that the angle of the sun and the temperature have changed just enough, and with the fact that you are just enough more tired this time to make that imperceptible difference in line, judgment, and reaction time. Take heart. I promise you'll do better in the morning. Maybe right after that no-count first run.

9 *Powder*

Skiing in fresh powder has been described in terms ranging from "excruciating" to "erotic." Surely it is the snow condition most eulogized in skiing literature and films. But it's the old story: what is euphoria for one is an agonizing struggle with fear and the wrong set of muscles for another. Some literally come floating down cloudlike fields of untracked fluff, while others wallow in it, picking the white stuff out of their goggles and longjohns. Some pretty good skiers avoid it entirely.

If you know just a few things about skiing in it, powder is nothing to be afraid of. Always remember that technique is far more important than brute strength. Here are two basic things to keep in mind—one good and one bad.

On the bad side: there is lots of resistance to your skis turning. You have probably already discovered that the deeper and heavier the snow becomes, the worse this gets. You are going to have to work harder at un-

134

weighting. You are also going to have to develop skills which will give you added "torque" when you need it.

On the good side: while there is lots of resistance to your skis changing direction, there is lots of resistance to your going very fast. The snow slows you. This means that you can take a more "aggressive" line on any slope than you might take on a normal day. You don't need to turn so sharply to control your speed, so you can stay closer to the fall line as you make gentle turns.

Skiing in powder is largely a matter of faith. If you believe that the snow is going to keep you from going too fast, you will learn to do well. If you don't believe it, you are in trouble, and will continue to struggle and wallow.

If your psyche seems to keep getting in your way after there has been a good snowfall—visions of injury-suspended family or business responsibilities loom before your mind's eye—get out early one morning and have a run on some easy intermediate slope before it gets packed. Schuss at first, just to feel the snow holding you back. Just relax. Then try making some *very* gentle turns—only a few degrees away from the fall line. When you get to the bottom, turn around and admire the pattern made by your tracks. If this backward glance suddenly turns you on—and I think it will—you are off and running. You'll be a good powder skier in no time at all.

The best way to ski in powder is to sit back, right?

I am asked this question at least once each day there has been new snow. The idea that you always sit back in powder snow is a myth. Much of the time new powder has fallen on top of hard base. Your tips might disappear beneath the surface of the snow—this is only scary; not dangerous—but they cannot "dive" in 4 to 6 inches of snow. Where there has been a moderate amount of new snow on a previously packed surface, you will ski best if you *don't* alter your normal skiing stance too much.

Granted, in very light, "bottomless" powder, it *is* dangerous to let your ski tips get very deep beneath the surface. To keep them up, you might want to stand more flat-footed, lower your fanny a little, and straighten your back a bit. This will make you feel as though you are balancing on your skis' tails.[1]

Why do I have such a hard time getting started in powder?

Because you are a little frightened and are forgetting how important that first turn is. Probably you are trying to start by skiing across the hill. You need tremendous physical strength to make the first turn from a traverse. It takes a certain amount of *mental* fortitude to point your skis right down the fall line first, but that's what works best. Screw up your courage and point them *downhill* before you do anything.

You may be surprised at how slowly you build up speed. You will have plenty of time to think. You may discover that you can ski the very steepest slopes with this line as long as the powder lasts.

Don't make your first turn too soon. A little speed helps in powder. All of your turns should be gradual ones. Don't wrestle with your inability to turn sharply. It won't hurt you to spend a little more time in the fall line.

What's the best way to unweight in powder?

"Down-up" is clearly the most effective. Anticipation is good too if the snow is not to heavy. "Rebound" is almost impossible in soft snow; so

---

[1] The wording in this description of a good deep-powder stance is taken from Joubert, p. 100, and from Abraham, p. 37.

jet turns are pretty much out. "Squatty-body" turns work well; down un-weighting does not. Pushing your feet down into the depths of the snow can get you hung up. Retracting the legs, on the other hand, can help you ski over the surface.[2]

All unweighting movements should be emphasized. They *must* flow together smoothly. Fluid "total motion" is imperative. Any sudden, abrupt motions can get you into trouble.

If you edge sharply, you merely compress or roll the snow beneath your edges, tripping yourself. Keep your skis as flat as you can and still make the turn.[3]

How much should I worry about what is beneath the surface?

If you like to ski "out of bounds," there is always the danger of hidden rocks, holes, crevices, and stumps. Even if you stay within the normal confines of a ski area, you should at least be thinking about what is underneath.

A little bit of powder on top of glare ice can catch you by surprise. Drifts are hard to see. The snow is more dense in a drift, but it looks the same. Skiing into it can slow you suddenly and cause a fall.

A breeze can drift light fresh snow into the troughs between moguls, making a field of bumps look deceptively smooth. Don't be fooled. Try to *feel* the bumps even if you cannot see them. They are still there. Ski slowly and alertly enough so that when a disguised bump gives you a lift, you can turn there.

New snow tends to round off bumps as well as make the troughs less

[2] Abraham, p. 36.
[3] Joubert, pp. 100–102.

137

sharp. You don't need to worry quite so much about the hazards of "impossible" moguls.

Are there any other adjustments I should make?

I have to contradict a remark I made in the last chapter, by saying that you should consciously try to keep your feet together in powder. Normally this is a bad approach. But if you let a stream of snow pass between your feet, it tends to force your feet farther and farther apart as you gain speed.

Trying to use independent leg action can cause problems. If you get your skis even slightly out of parallel, they both seem to want to continue in their respective nonparallel lines. I'm sure you don't need to be told that this can result either in crossed tips or in a "spread eagle," unless you can correct yourself quickly. Never stem or snowplow in powder.

How do I stop?!

Stopping *can* be a real problem! When you are in motion, the reason for the more aggressive line is to keep you from exposing the whole length of your skis sideways to the snow. This is why you always try to keep your skis pointed basically at the fall line. But when you stop, you must make a completed turn. More often than any of us like to admit, we catch the outside edge at this point, and fall over.

You need *very* little edge in powder. You certainly don't need angulation. So stop by making a gradual, finished, *banked* turn, with your skis quite flat. This way you will be less apt to fall downhill when you stop. In fact, banking is usually a good way to ski in powder.

I still have my weight on the outside ski, don't I?

Weight *both* skis as much as you can. As you turn, some small portion of your weight can go to the outside ski, but the weight shift should be ever so subtle. Make a quick move from one ski to the other, and you are likely to end up on your ear.

Inward lean—banking—can be accompanied by weighting the *inside* ski. Bank, hook your inside knee (so that you put the ski slightly on its edge), and weight it.[4] Keep the downhill ski edged the same amount so that it doesn't continue in a straight line.

What about my hands?

Hold your hands higher than normal in powder, but where you can still see them. Following through more forcefully with the outer arm can help. Swing the arm in a high arc, like a reluctant roundhouse punch.[5] This is also a contradiction of a point I made earlier, in Chapter 4, but sometimes in powder you need all the turning power you can get.

If you are banking a lot, the outside hand will be somewhat higher than the inside hand. Plant your pole gently. If you really jab with it, and the snow is deep, it might sink in up to its grip! That will slow you down in a real hurry. Lots of good powder skiers do not put their hands through their pole straps for just this reason. This has probably prevented a few broken wrists. If you rely too much on your poles to help you balance, you will learn *not* to in deep powder!

[4] This hooking motion is called *cramponnage* by the French. See Joubert, p. 104.
[5] Abraham, p. 37.

FIGURE 25: *Linked turns in powder snow with hip projection.* Experienced ski teachers frequently cringe when they hear other skiers giving each other technical advice. All too often it becomes a case of the blind leading the blind. But not long ago I overheard a fellow trying to help a friend who was *obviously* struggling in new powder snow. "Seymour," he said, "Pretend you're a big hairy bird! Glide! Float on the currents. Don't fight it so much." Good advice, I thought.

Here we see our demonstrator floating, more or less like such a bird, through powder (also through something of a blizzard). He is trying to remain very relaxed and light on his feet; trying to feel the harder surface beneath the fresh snow.

1. In the first figure we can see that he is almost banking—trying not to weight either the inside ski or the outside ski too much. He pushes his feet down until he can feel some solid resistance underneath.

2. Then he retracts his legs, unweighting with *avalement* . . .

3. . . . and *projects* or throws his hips slightly to the outside of the turn to give himself extra turning power. Notice how the outside arm swings to lend added rotary motion and torque.

4. Now the legs *steer*—very gingerly—through the turn . . .

5. . . . and the hips are projected to the outside again.

6. Although the hands are held somewhat higher than they might normally be, notice the by-now-familiar athletic stance. The skier is still on the balls of his feet (not sitting back), ready to move in any direction depending on the state of the snow, his speed (which has to do with his state of mind), and whatever is happening beneath his feet in terms of bumps and holes.

140

How can I get more turning power when I need it?

Use another one of the "no-no's" I have preached against. Let your hips rotate a little! When hip rotation is okay, it is called "hip projection." It should be used only in powder, in crud . . . and in moderation.

When you are in the fall line, push your hips to the outside of the turn (#2–#3, #6–#7 in Fig. 25) and rotate them slightly—pointing your belly button the way you are trying to go. You might find yourself doing this as you make the second down motion with your knees.

As you wedel in powder, you will keep throwing your hip to one side and then the other.[6] It will look like you are doing a restrained hula in slow motion. (In this case watch the hips, not the hands.)

Try not to overdo any of these motions, either with your hands or your torso. Balance is as much a problem in powder as it is any other time. Any excess can throw you off.

Why do I have so much trouble on a slope that is partially skied out?

Because the parts that are skied out are fast—there is no soft snow to hold you back—and the unpacked places are still slow. You are constantly accelerating and decelerating without meaning to. Turn more completely where there is a packed spot; less where the snow is still fluffy.

Clumps of soft snow, built up by turning skis but not yet hardened into moguls, can be tricky. If you allow yourself any slippage at all, so that you hit them sideways, you are probably going to fall. Approach them head-on, and "blast" through them directly without letting your skis get turned sideways. Keep your feet together.

If you must turn in a clump, anticipation seems to work the best. In

[6] Joubert, p. 102.

fact, it can look very impressive (see Fig. 26). But be careful not to project your upper body so far downhill that you fall on your face if your feet don't break out of the soft snow as soon as you expect. This has happened to me more than once—with a class right behind me!

Should I have special skis for powder?

The skis you have are probably fine if they are not too stiff or too narrow, and are not a particularly "turny" pair of slalom skis. If you are going to be skiing where there is often a lot of powder, a special pair of "deep powder" skis might be a good idea. If you can afford only one extra pair of skis, and you live in the eastern U. S. or Canada for example, a ski that is good on ice might be a better investment.

Good powder skis are wide—especially in the shovel section—and relatively soft. The flex pattern is uniform—the skis are not a great deal stiffer in some places and softer in others, but will flex evenly throughout their length. Most modern skis are being engineered more or less this way, and most of them are satisfactory in powder.

Any other suggestions for powder skiing?

Falling in deep powder is soft, fun, and usually safe. Don't be so afraid of falling that you are unable to relax and ski well. Being carefree and loose is one of the essential psychological elements in good powder skiing. Don't forget that it is hard work. You will get more tired than you might on a normal day.

It's fun to ski with friends on powder days. You can ooh and ahh about each other's tracks. A companion can be a welcome sight when you fall. Sometimes it's awfully hard to get up by yourself, especially if one ski comes off.

143

FIGURE 26: *Braking in powder snow*. On packed or hard snow most of us control our speed by turning our skis well out of the fall line and setting an edge. This is bad technique for powder-snow skiing—particularly when the powder is partially skied out and the snow is more concentrated in some spots than it is in others. Turn too far *across* the slope and you will get hung up—especially if you try to weight the downhill ski instead of weighting both skis more or less equally.

One friend of mine—a real Western powder expert—happily admitted to me, "When the snow gets built up into big clumps, I point my skis straight downhill, build up a lot of speed until I am nearly out of control, and then start looking for mounds of soft snow to ski into and slow myself down."

Few of us have the courage to ski very steep powder runs with this sort of near-reckless abandon. But the point is well worth making: turning in powder is used less for braking and more for changing direction to seek out soft bumps or snow-filled holes which can be used for slowing down. Be constantly on the look-out for places where the snow is the deepest. These spots offer the most resistance to excessively high speeds.

You will be amazed at how much you can check your speed by blasting into soft moguls in a low crouch and making a gentle squatty-body turn using *avalement*. Snow will fly up against your legs, your bottom, your chest—sometimes even into your face so you can't breath for a second. But to some—including me—this is one of skiing's biggest thrills. Try it. When you see how effectively you can slow down this way, greater speeds in powder snow won't seem quite so scary.

144

But don't try to follow close behind someone else. His skis will throw up a lot of snow (see Fig. 27). Skiing in his "rooster tail," you won't be able to see a thing.

Spend some time and money and find yourself a pair of goggles that work on powdery days—ones that won't fog even when you get sweaty. There are some good ones on the market. Some skiers—I for one—prefer good sunglasses that allow lots of cool air to get between the lenses and your face, which inhibits fogging.

Do you know that a baseball cap or golf hat with a visor keeps falling snow out of your goggles or glasses? It's comfortable on warm days too, because it acts as a sweatband on your head. It also shades your eyes from the harsh spring sun.

Plan to get out early when it looks like there will be new snow. In many areas fresh powder is gone by eleven o'clock because it is rolled by machinery and the good skiers have gotten out onto it early.

Is powder skiing really all it's cracked up to be?

Yes, although if there were nothing but powder, skiing would soon get boring. Even skiing with someone else, powder skiing can be a soulfully private, quiet, sensuous experience. Have you noticed how skis make no sound in powder? On regular days they scrape and grind.

A friend and I rode the chairlift very early in the morning one dark and snowy day last winter. We were both sleepy and didn't say much on

FIGURE 27: Once you have the confidence to really "get it on" in powder snow, you will probably find that those especially white winter mornings (when there are very few ski tracks) just don't happen often enough—even in a place like Utah. When you begin to feel this way, you are well on your way to becoming a "powder hound."

146

147

the ride up. When we got to the top, he started down first. He made two nice turns, whistled softly to himself, and kept skiing. I watched him for a long time until I couldn't see him any more in the falling snow.

I followed, avoiding his tracks. I too skied for a long, long, long time before the spell was broken by the pain in my legs, and I reluctantly pulled up in front of his grinning figure. "Dennis," I started to say.

"Don't say anything. You'll spoil it," he said and pointed his tips downhill again. We had three more runs before the morning class. I don't know if there was anyone else on the mountain, and couldn't have cared less. I guess this is what skiing is all about.

10 *Ice*

Ice is the final test. Have you noticed how the very good skier makes skiing on it look easy? One of the astonishing things about the *great* skier, in fact, is that he looks very much the same regardless of the conditions. One of your goals should be this kind of consistency.

There is lots of good skiing to be had on ice. It comes in three basic grades, with lots of variations in texture and hardness. "Blue ice"—sometimes called "black ice"—has a very high water content. It is something like what hockey teams play on. Even the super experts steer clear of this. Fortunately it is usually patchy, shiny, and easy to see. It rarely covers a whole mountain. If you have to ski over blue ice, spread your feet apart, ski straight ahead, and hope for a better place to turn on the other side.

"Gray ice" and "frozen granular" are better. Racers ski on this all the time, and seem to thrive. Gray ice is harder and more slippery than granular. Granular tends to be crunchy and brittle. It has the least amount

149

of water content. The important thing they both have in common is that you *can* set an edge in them if you know what you are doing, and if your equipment is in good shape.

As a New England Yankee trying to make the best of a bad situation (erratic weather patterns over the Northeast bring us more than our share of ice), I have long been an advocate of ice skiing as the best way to improve your technique.

Look at it this way: lots of good skiers can look good on those ideal days. On packed powder, you *can* get away with the sort of "technical murder" we have discussed—even in bumps. On ice you get away with very little. This can be humiliating, especially if you are already a very good skier. All too often the temptation is to spend your hard-earned weekend in the baselodge bar. (The bars do a great business on icy days.) After all, why should you have to go out and bounce your bottom down some silly ice-encrusted mountain?

The nice thing about ice—if anything good can be said about it—is that it magnifies and amplifies your smallest mistakes. Improvement is impossible whenever mistakes don't show. Remember that learning never stops. Rid yourself of the comfortable-base-lodge syndrome and come out and play. I don't think you'll be sorry.

Where are the best places to ski on icy days?

You will probably want to stay away from the very steepest slopes at first. You may find that lesser ones offer challenge enough. Any loose snow blown by wind over the surface of a slope can polish ice and make it icier. Look for places that are sheltered from the wind.

Choose some "road less traveled by." It is most slippery wherever there has been the heaviest traffic. You have probably learned that the edges of a trail can be less icy than the middle, because fewer people skied

ICE

there before it got icy. But do you remember that there is relatively soft snow (ice) on the tops of bumps? Turn there.

If it was slushy the day before, and now there are frozen mounds, ruts, and ski tracks, stay more toward the middle of the slope again. It is usually smoother there. Frozen ruts are catchy and "chattery." Vibrations in your legs which come as you try to "hold" on this stuff will make your legs very tired. Unweight with a hop if you have to, to prevent your skis from getting directed off course by a frozen track.

I shouldn't "hop" on ice, should I?

No, only on frozen "crud." Normally ice, by definition, is smooth and slick. On ice it is easier to turn than not to turn. This can result in what is called "overturning."

Unweight as gently as possible, as though you were skiing on eggs. If you are going to use a conventional parallel turn, come up ever so softly, but make your down motion *hard!* The problem on ice is just the opposite of the problem on powder: you don't worry about turning too little; you try not to turn too *far.* Down unweighting, as I've said, works best on ice. Sink and edge in the same motion (see Fig. 28).

Your psychological stategy must change on ice too. In powder it helps to be something of a blithe spirit. On ice you will want to be more pensive and deliberate. All of your edging motions will have to be made with great precision. Always try to be conscious of how the consistency of the ice is changing. Sometimes you can hear a difference in the sound your edges make.

How should ice affect my stance?

I would say that it is better to be too far forward than too far back. On the other hand, if you are pressing *too* far over your tips, you are not

151

Figure 28: *Turn on ice with upper-body angulation.* This series of pictures of a single high-speed turn on ice is reminiscent of the positions made famous years ago by the great Austrian ski schools. But there is one important difference: notice how there is little or none of the awkward "reverse shoulder" or "counter-rotary" position in the upper body. The upper body tilts to the outside to help get the center of the skier's body mass (weight) over the outside ski—the ski that is about to become the new downhill ski. Yet the shoulders still face essentially the way the skis are headed.

1. *Any* kind of unweighting that you use on ice should be done gently because the skis will change direction very easily—sometimes too easily, as you may have discovered. This particular turn was made with down unweighting. Here the demonstrator is still in a relatively high position, although at this point he has already changed edges from the previous traverse.

2. Now he has dropped to a lower position—driving his knees to the right. This leg action—exactly the same thing we have seen since the beginning of this book—has sometimes been called lower-body angulation. The upper body, in the meantime, also angulates—in the opposite direction. This helps the skier maintain balance and encourages the skis to carve.

3. Here the skis continue to carve even though the surface of this steep slope is very slippery. The head even is slightly on an angle. See how it tips slightly to the outside of the turn? This little bit of added weight helps the skis to "bite" at this very critical point in the turn.

4. Once the turn is fairly well completed the skier rises to a higher and less angulated position. Don't forget: you cannot down-unweight for very many turns if you never rise up *between* turns. You can't keep going down forever! In other words, you should begin down-unweighted turns from a fairly extended stance.

In spite of what some may say, "angulation" should not be considered a dirty word among modern skiers—particularly as one becomes more and more proficient. Study photos of how the racers ski if you need convincing. You will see that they frequently use the upper body to assist and counterbalance—but never interfere with—the lower body. Use angulation (without contorting counter-rotation) whenever you think it may be helpful.

152

using the full length of your edges as well as you could be. Ideally, you should be in a low "gorilla stance," standing right over the pivot point of your skis, trying to carve with both the tips and the tails.

Adopt a comfortable wide-track stance in your feet. Edge *both* skis. You should feel most of your weight along the inside length of your downhill foot. You should also feel some weight on the outside of your uphill foot. That's not nearly so complicated as it sounds. Notice how the best ice skiers who use this open stance—racers are a good example—sometimes look a little bowlegged.

How important are sharp edges, really?

On ice, nothing will work right if your equipment is poorly maintained—if your edges are rounded or burred, or if you have nicks, gouges, and scratches in your bottoms.

But edges can be a skier's scapegoat. More often than not, "dull" edges are blamed for lack of skiing success on icy days. Most of the time, the fault is more with technique and line than with faulty equipment. One of the most amusing ironies is that sometimes people who complain most bitterly about their edges don't use them properly enough to get them dull.

All other things being equal, the skier with sharper edges will do better, of course. A very good skier, like a good finish carpenter, is a fanatic about the sharpness of his tools. To him, skiing on ice with rounded edges is like trying to shave with a rusty razor blade. He may claim that he can feel the slightest imperfection in his edges and bottoms. He probably can.

Learn to maintain your skis yourself, or at least find a ski mechanic you can trust to keep them "tuned" properly for you. Keep them in mint condition. It's not that hard to do.[1]

---

[1] For a complete buying guide to ice-skiing equipment and directions for sharpening edges and fixing bottoms, see Stu Campbell, "The Challenge on Ice," *Skier's Digest* (Northbrook, Illinois: Digest Books, 1970), pp. 81–89.

154

ICE

Is there any way I can hold better on ice?

More angulation will help. But wait a minute: don't confuse angulation with counter-rotation. Drop one shoulder to get your weight over the downhill ski more, but keep facing the way you are going and keep both hands in sight.

To exaggerate angulation on ice, make believe that the pitch of every slope is greater than it is (see Fig. 29). On a normal day the natural tilt of the upper body should correspond to the steepness of the hill. The skier in Fig. 28 is pretending that the distance between the imaginary street and sidewalk is more than it actually is (see Chapter 2). If you were to draw a line across the tops of his shoulders, that line would look steeper than the horizon.

I can ski with angulation when there is good snow, all right, but not when it's icy!

Many *good* skiers have made this remark to me. Dropping that upper body to the outside of the turn is unnatural, there's no denying that, and the *idea* of doing it on ice is scary. But angulation does you no good where there is secure snow under you. Where it really helps is on ice.

What you are doing when you angulate, anatomically at least, is balancing the weight of your upper body on the top of your thigh bone.[2] When you do this, and drive your knees to put your skis on edge, you have tremendous gripping power because you have transmitted your weight and strength most efficiently to the edge of your downhill ski.

[2] Joubert, pp. 62, 115.

FIGURE 29: *Stance on ice.* Your stance on ice cannot be as relaxed and natural-looking as it might be on good packed powder snow. On ice try to edge both skis. Using two edges can be almost twice as effective as using one. If your feet come apart a little and you look slightly bowlegged, you are probably doing lots of things right.

Angulation on *good* snow conditions should be a "happening" which results from the fact that your downhill foot is slightly lower than your uphill foot at the end of each turn. In this case a line drawn across the top of the shoulders should be parallel to the pitch of the slope (see the middle line in the illustration).

On ice it is important to get weight over the outside ski—the one that is becoming the new downhill ski. This may mean that the body is tilted *more* than the slope as each turn is completed.

That sounds too technical. I'm still not convinced.

It's simply a matter of standing up or falling down. Take your pick. What was it we learned from Isaac Newton in high-school physics about "equal and opposite reactions" to preserve balance?

Your upper body has to counterbalance what your lower body does. If your knees bend to one side, and you lean the same way, you will fall down. Try it standing still. The upper body has to "angulate" the opposite way (see Fig. 28 again).

If you water ski, if you ride a bicycle, or if you are not used to skiing on ice, this idea is hard to accept at first. On a bike, if you want to turn to the left, you turn the handlebars to the left, and lean left. But skiing on ice, if you want to turn to the left, you push your *knees* left, and lean right! Don't forget: it's the right ski that is the turning ski. Angulation means that you must lean what seems to be the wrong way. Banking, incidentally, is clearly not a good idea on ice, for just this reason.

When I angulate to one side, I can really feel my skis bite, but I can't seem to do it on the other side. Why?

This isn't unusual. Lots of very good skiers are basically one-footed. Sometimes skiers who have been injured favor one foot. Perhaps if you could, you would like always to ski on, say, your right ski, regardless of which way you were turning. This feeling is not conscious, of course.

You might angulate beautifully when you make a turn to the left. That's the good side if you are right-footed. When you turn to the right, you *think* that you are leaning left, but you are still leaning to the right a little. This is most apt to happen when you link turns together and get confused. Every time you turn left, you slow down. Every time you turn right, you accelerate.

157

How do I correct this?

Gymnasts know how important the head can be when it comes to balance. Something like one-seventh of your weight is located in your head. To experience what good angulation feels like on your bad side, lay your head right down on your outside shoulder until your ear touches. If your head gets tipped over this way while you turn, everything else seems to tip too, and you will have good angulation. Once you know what it feels like to have your skis really grip on ice, hold your head erect again while your body stays tilted. It's hard to keep your balance if you are looking at the world sideways.

That's probably more than enough about angulation. You may already use it effectively. As boots get higher and higher, and as ski design improves, angulation will go the way of bamboo poles and rope tows. Until then, use it when you need it. It's a valuable body position.

I should take a more conservative line on ice, right?

People think I have lost my marbles when I tell them to pick a more aggressive line on ice. Flat traverses—even *very* short ones—invite trouble and fatigue on icy days. Holding *any* line can be hard work.

Lots of quick determined turns right down the fall line are more effective than longer, completed ones. It is better to make a brief but forceful edgeset than to try to gri-i-i-i-nd your way through a long-radius turn. Watch a good racer in an icy slalom. *Listen* to his skis. To turn, he will not edge for a long time, the way you might expect. He hits his edges— WHAM!—and then gets *off* them. He is edging just long enough to check his speed a bit, and change direction. You don't need to go as fast as he does, but you should use his edging tactics. Your skis will make the same distinct cutting sound when you are turning well on ice.

158

ICE

What do I do when I can't seem to hold at all?

Where it is very slippery and your edges seem to "wash out" on you, don't waste your strength fighting it too much. Start a new turn right away. If you can't grip then, turn again. Take advantage of the fact that it *is* easy to turn on ice, even if it is hard to hold. Continual turning slows you some.

On ice you are going to sideslip more than you do on good snow. Don't worry about it. Don't worry too much about abrupt, jerky motions, either. On ice you simply cannot be so gracefully serpentine.

How can I keep from overturning?

Turning so far out of the fall line that your tips are pointed too far uphill is one of the hazards of ice skiing. Overturning destorys your rhythm and makes getting into the next turn very awkward. It can be caused by even the slightest hip rotation.

If your hips are very still, you may be overturning because you are standing on your edges too long and your tails are "washing out." Attack the ice! Lower your fanny, stick those knees out in front of you, and "turn on." *Hit* your edges, get off them, and *hit* them again! No Casper Milquetoast ever skied well on ice.

What about icy moguls?

Use anticipation and rebound wherever you can get a solid edgeset. Keep checking against the uphill side of moguls, turn, slide through the trough, hit your edges on the next flat "step," and turn again. I have heard skiing in icy moguls described as a series of carefully controlled sideslips and edgesets. That's all it is.

Plant your pole like you mean it—far enough away from you so that you don't slide into it sideways and trip yourself. If you are too dainty with your pole plant, the tip of the pole can skid and throw you off. If you do get off balance in the icy bumps, don't fight too long for recovery, and build up a dangerous amount of speed. Fall to stop if you have to. Few serious accidents happen to expert skiers on icy days. There is no soft snow to catch a ski and give your leg a twist. All you do is bounce and slide.

Above all: be the *boss* when it is icy! Remember that moguls are formed on days when there is slower, softer snow. You can not accept their natural rhythm on icy days or you will get going much too fast. Turn more frequently then the bumps seem to demand. Watch the good ice skiers again. They know that when they get into a tight spot, they have to make *more* turns—not fewer. You might come to a particularly big mogul, discover that it is really glassy there, and have to make *three* turns down its backside to control your speed. The sooner you believe in the value of the brief, hard edgeset on ice, the more fun you are going to have.

Anything else?

Skiing on ice can be fun for a few days. When it stays icy for weeks on end, even professional skiers start dreaming of hot beaches. Usually it doesn't. The really miserable days are becoming a rarity. Ski-area operators are installing more and more snow-making guns, and are buying dragging devices that pulverize the ice, making a surface that is quite pleasant to ski on. They are obviously determined to cut into the icy-day profits of the local bars, and to make the ski business less risky.

Still, lift lines vanish on icy days. As you get better and better, and venture out onto more and more "impossible" conditions, you may one day discover that you have suddenly become a member of an elite group of diehard skiers. What percentage of the total skiing population can go out

160

on a very icy day and do *well?* And how many of them are out there this day?

Others out there may not say much to you, but they are watching. Late in the loneliness of the afternoon they are comforted by the sound of your skis scraping somewhere on another part of the mountain. They know you are there. A strange camaraderie, that.

And at the end of a particularly icy day—even if you are a little bruised—there is no feeling quite the same as meeting a group of friends who *have* stayed inside all day, and have not even bothered to put on their boots.

"How was it?" they laugh.

"Good," you say. And mean it.

11 *Odds and Ending*

Ski mainly for yourself, not for the benefit of someone who might be watching. Now that you are good enough to "ski with the big boys," and no longer have to worry about mastering technique, it is time to find your own unique style. Skiing is no longer a question of competing with others as much as it is learning to deal with yourself and with those natural forces—like gravity and cold and fear—over which you have little control. Now the point is learning not to defeat the mountain, but to synchronize yourself with it.

Yet unless you own your own mountain, you can never ski entirely by yourself. There will always be others around. Most of them will not ski as well as you do. And always there will be a few who are better. This is as it should be. After all, without other "big boys," how else are we to measure ourselves and our accomplishments?

Every very good skier, however humble in temperament, craves that rare and splendid time when he is the best skier on the hill. I am sure you crave it too: that unexpected and incomparable moment when you ski over a rise and all action below you pauses as others there wait to watch you pass, and even good skiers on the lift turn their heads to see you a moment longer. Such hesitation—to study another skier as he passes—is the ultimate compliment, the wordless expression of admiration among very good skiers. I hope you are one of those I turn my head to watch.

Such a run should bring personal satisfaction, but never conceit. You can never let being the momentary center of attention go to your head. On the next run it will be you who will pause to watch someone else. And when you try to emulate his style, you may fall, literally, flat on your face. It's as simple as that. Never underestimate the sport's capacity to put you in your place.

Is there any point in my taking lessons now?

Yes and double yes. It has never been my intention to degrade ski instruction. It is a fine profession that makes constant efforts to improve itself and offer excellent instruction. Don't try to learn from your friends. Your friends may be very fine skiers and they may have the best intentions in the world, but all they do, usually, is teach you their bad habits. Find a good instructor—a good ski *teacher.*

Any instructor who is certified by a reputable examining organization is theoretically qualified to teach anyone, any place, any time, on any level. But just any certified instructor may not suit your needs as a very good skier.

Any top ski school has several instructors who are particularly qualified to teach on a very advanced, sophisticated level. Because of their vast experience, their understanding of people as well as technique, and their skiing ability, they are in great demand, and you will see them skiing for fun only rarely. But they are among the biggest boys on *any* mountain.

It is easy enough to find out who they are. Ask the ski-school direc-tor. If you don't trust his judgment, ask some of the local people who are also very good skiers. Sometimes they know best.

Should I take class lessons or private lessons?

Class lessons can be a lot of fun. Generally the higher you get in a ski school, the smaller the classes become. Instructors have to keep reminding themselves, though, that people are skiing for fun, not to spend several hours with a drill sergeant. Class lessons cannot be overly intensive for just this reason, but if you get into a class with a homogeneous group, you can learn a lot.

On Monday morning of a "ski week" (where you spend several days with the same class and the same instructor), a good ski school will spend lots of time watching people ski and sorting them into the right groups. This can be very frustrating for the very good skier who is champing at the bit. In a "ski week" class, the members of the group have a great deal to say about what direction the class will take as far as how much "fun" and how much "work" there will be. Stick around during the class "splitting." It's worth the wait!

People learn to ski in plateaus. Some are easy to reach, others harder for some people. If you have a specific problem or are trying to get over a particularly difficult plateau, try a private lesson. Any instructor worth his salt should be able to teach you more in one hour than in a week of class lessons. He'll give you enough to think about and practice for days.

Private lessons are expensive. Nearly always they are worth it. But once in a while, I think, people expect too much. An instructor is not a magician. What he is teaching you may not work for you in the space of one hour. Sometimes things may not gel for two or three days. So be sure you understand what he is telling you. There's nothing sadder than watch-ing a skier trying to do something he apparently doesn't understand. Don't

164

be self-conscious. Ask questions. Encourage him to explain another way and show you again. It's his job to be patient, and he wants you to get your money's worth.

But will a ski instructor teach me what I want to learn?

Ski-school directors sometimes get complaints from people who say they were not taught what they wanted to be taught. I am sure there are doctors who will treat a patient for whatever ailment he thinks he has, just as I am sure that there are ski instructors who will teach jet turns to someone who still needs work on basic christies.

A good instructor will examine your skiing before he tells you anything. Don't be afraid to communicate with him, but let him be the doctor. Let *him* diagnose your problems and offer solutions. That's what he is trained to do. You might be surprised at how quickly he can correct your little mistakes and bring you along to what you wanted to learn in the first place.

How should I choose a private instructor?

I have joked with skiers who were frightened or reluctant to do what I suggest by saying, "Look, there are three people in life you *have* to trust: your doctor, your lawyer, and your ski instructor." I am always half serious. Again, choose an instructor for his reputation as a teacher first, for his personal skiing style second. If he is really good he can ski any style you want. Find someone who is compatible and flexible—someone you can level with.

Above all, don't be put off by some of the bad publicity ski instruction has been getting in recent years. A few instances of bad instruction should not hurt the whole profession—especially the real "big boys." Skiing has grown at a phenomenal rate. So has the number of very good skiers. There is no doubt that there have not been enough really good instructors to keep up with the demands of the expert skiers. The clientele of a particular area tends to get what it demands. In some places less qualified instructors are hired to entertain vast hordes of snow bunnies who arrive in busloads. In other places, where there are lots of good skiers, you will find super-pros to teach them. Go where the big boys go if you want the best instruction.

Should I spend a lot of time skiing with my family?

I think that most families—or couples—who try to ski together are crazy. So are parents who try to teach their children. Nine times out of ten, they all end up fighting, and this is enough to ruin the day for everyone. Here is where you can take advantage of the ski school.

Ski and take lessons separately. Instructors cringe when a couple makes a request to take a private lesson together. Almost never are the two of equal ability, and almost always one is embarrassed—often the husband. Don't hold yourself or any member of your family back—*particularly* a teen-ager. Let everyone progress—or not—at his own rate, and agree to meet for lunch.

Why haven't you said anything about jumps and trick skiing?

Jumps and tricks are to expert skiing what the Harlem Globe Trotters are to professional basketball. Royal christies, "outrigger turns," and "splits" are fun to do. I have never done a flip, although it is fun to watch others. But all of these things are really beside the point. They are elements of style rather than technique.

166

ODDS AND ENDING

Some ski schools attract people to their advanced classes by offering to teach tricks. What they are doing, essentially, is admitting that after a certain point they run out of challenging terrain to interest the very good skier. So they offer a different kind of challenge. This is great.

Some areas have a trick-skiing specialist on their staff. He may give demonstrations, enter professional "hot dog" contests, and teach a special "fun" or "freestyle" class. These are very popular. He may even coach a junior freestyle team. This seems like a good alternative for a gifted young skier who is not interested in racing.

What is a "pure" carved turn?

The concept of the "pure" carved turn is described by a neighbor of mine in a book called *How the Racers Ski*. His name is Warren Witherell and he does a fine job of training junior racers at Burke Mountain Academy, not far from Stowe. Warren insists that a racer, in order to be really competitive, must be able to change direction without losing any speed at all.

In a perfectly executed carved turn, there is absolutely no sideways slippage. The entire length of the ski's edge passes over the *exact* same spot on the snow. If you look at the mark left in the snow, you should see that the track is never wider than the width of the ski. An average racer or good recreational skier, according to Warren, will start his skis turning and then put them on edge. In a pure carved turn—which only some racers are able to do—the ski is put on edge first, and *then* turned.

Some very experienced ski technicians have called *How the Racers Ski* a radical and "impossible" approach to racing. I am not sure that I would go that far because I think I have occasionally felt what Warren is talking about. He is asking his own racers to strive for an ideal turn—which, of course, he should be. But I question the ability of even a top flight racer to sustain the technique he describes for more than a few turns. *How the Racers Ski* is well worth reading, though. Warren points out, incidentally—with the help of excellent photographs by Malcolm Reiss (who also took the pictures for this book)—that it is the young teen-age racers who are the best technical skiers in the world! I think he is right.

I have a twelve-year-old who thinks he would like to race. Should he?

Of course! Learning to race will be fun and will improve his skiing immeasurably. If your child is already twelve, he may be starting a little late if he has National Team or Olympic Team aspirations. But that should not discourage him from joining a junior racing program. Both you and he should be prepared to make a pretty total commitment to it, though.

I was a junior racing coach for several years, and I know the tremendous physical and psychological pressure junior racers can be under. Skiing has to be an all-consuming passion for a youngster if he is to do well even on the junior circuit. The competition is fierce.

You should also be warned that junior racing is falling under the same sort of criticism as is Little League baseball. Racing teams can turn into the worst sort of "Pushy Parents Clubs." Fortunately both parents and coaches are becoming more understanding, and are relaxing the programs for the youngest kids, putting more emphasis on learning and less emphasis on winning or even on making a spot on the team. This seems to be producing fewer emotional casualties, and perhaps it will allow us to bring along even better racers in even greater numbers.

Should I try racing?

Sure. It will do a lot for *your* skiing too, and will add to your total understanding of the sport. Skiing through gates forces you to think ahead, turn in a given spot, and learn precise edge control. Ski-club and ski-bum races, and NASTAR competition, usually involve a high level of very good skiers. It's fun to pit yourself against your friends, and interesting to compare your time to that of a forerunner—or "pace setter" as they are sometimes called—who is a super expert. What is most fun of all is trying to figure out how you can be going all out, and *still* the forerunner beats you by four full seconds.

What do you think about the various short ski methods of teaching, like GLM?

As a very good skier, GLM (Graduated Length Method) is not for you, of course. It is a means to an end you have already achieved. It is another effort on the part of ski schools to help people to ski sooner and with less effort and frustration. It is no gimmick.

I do not go for the idea of starting people on *very* short skis (90 centimeters). I think that it is important for everyone to learn an effective braking snowplow and to learn how to turn his skis properly. The real "shorties" make it too easy to cheat and develop bad habits that will hurt later on. They also result in lots of backward falls because there is no tail behind the foot to steady the skier.

Most American schools have accepted the 160-centimeter ski as the minimum length to start with. This is easy for most adults to turn on most kinds of snow, has good stability, and forces a beginner to use his legs and feet to turn correctly from the beginning. Once he has mastered that length, he should go right on to something longer. Encourage your friends to try this approach.

What is the "hot" ski this winter?

I wish that this didn't seem so important to so many people. As a very good skier you should rely on your own judgment rather than on fad, or on what all the other good skiers are using. There are many fine skis on the market. The best ones are expensive, so you should choose carefully.

There are many models of skis under one brand name. This can be confusing. You should be considering the top-performance skis in each line. Too many skiers are afraid of a competition model because they think it will be "hard to turn." This is nonsense! No racer is going to ski on anything that makes turning difficult. He wants the smoothest, most efficient-turning ski he can find. The so-called "combination" models are usually not designed with the very good skier in mind.

There is no reason to buy blind these days. Most ski shops near major ski areas have "demos" that you can try for a small fee. If you still have trouble making a decision, an instructor who knows your skiing intimately can probably offer good advice.

If you have not bought skis in the last three or four years, you might want to consider a pair that is 5 to 10 centimeters shorter than your old ones. GLM has apparently influenced this shorter-ski trend. Shorter skis are being designed for bigger folks. Give yourself a break.

What about boots?

I have always said that good boots are more important than good skis. It is still true. Boots should be your most cautious skiing investment. Plastic boots are here to stay. So are high backs and "canting"—adjusting the boots to compensate for knockknees or bowleggedness.

Be sure that the boots fit! Plastic boots do not stretch and break in. I like the sign I see in some ski shops that says, "Don't ask for a size. Ask to be fitted." Foaming can solve a lot of difficult fitting problems. Once they get the bugs out of the foaming process, *it* will be here to stay.

What's the best technique in the world—French, American, Austrian, what?

That's a loaded question, and I don't really know the answer. There is something to be said for each. I *do* know that a country's international racing record has very little to do with the teaching methods in its national ski school.

I am fairly well persuaded that the Austrians still know more about teaching skiing than anyone else in the world, although their teaching sequence, until very recently, has seemed painfully slow and overly methodical. The French seem to go to the opposite extreme—minimizing the importance of the traditional skiing fundamentals. The French emphasize skiing more and "correct position" less. Countries like Japan, Canada, Italy, and the United States seem to be gradually finding a good happy medium.

I hope that in a few years teaching methods throughout the world will be uniform and up-to-date, and so many people won't feel they have to ask this question.

Why are you a ski instructor?

To fulfill an aesthetic need, I guess. Certainly to fulfill a teaching need, an outdoor need, and to satisfy an addictive fascination with wintertime and skiable mountains. I have never had a romantic image of myself as dashing ski instructor. The job, like any other, is not without its frustrations and hassles.

I make a living, but I am not getting rich. I feel guilty about this sometimes. But not for long. All I have to do is remind myself of all the people who live where they don't really like living and do things they don't really like doing five days a week so that they can have enough money to do on weekends what I get paid to do all week.

What do you do in the summer?

The perennial question! I sail and play tennis for fun. I have built houses, been an English teacher and a graduate student. Much of the time I find myself waiting for winter, although I don't have much desire to travel the world in an endless-winter search.

Last spring I went back to school after the end of the skiing season. From the parking lot at the University of Vermont in Burlington, I could spend a moment each morning watching the snow line recede up the backside of Mt. Mansfield. It disappeared just as the lowest slopes were turning green.

And in the fall, several of us built a house in Stowe village. Professional skiers, all of us, we are supposedly immune to the tourist's premature excitement about the approach of winter. But when we went up to finish the roof one lazily crisp red-and-yellow autumn morning, somebody pointed back to the top of the mountain where there was a dusting of new early snow. We knew it would be melted by noon, but somehow the work quickened to keep pace with our quickened pulses. Suddenly, I think, we were worried about getting sailboats pulled out of Lake Champlain and about having the house completed by winter. . . . Of course we were ready for it long before the lifts opened for the season.

Don't you ever get sick of skiing?

No.

172

Index

173

INDEX

175

INDEX